KAREL H

LEARNING TO WALK

While her six-year-old son with special needs struggles to walk, this author's own struggle with alcoholism and eating disorders leads her down paths paved with grace, mercy and purpose.

outskirts press

Dedicated to Bob, whose unwavering love and encouragement helped me see myself as God sees me. Your dedication to providing for our family allowed me the space for our boys, my recovery and the work of Adam's Camp. You are a grace-of-God gift.

Introduction/Foreword

ORIGINALLY, I WANTED to write this book to chronicle the history of Adam's Camp. I co-founded Adam's Camp in 1986 to provide therapy programs for children with special needs and their families. The soul of any good organization lies in its roots, and losing that history can threaten the integrity of the mission. But the longer I thought about "the Adam's Camp story," the more I realized that this story is informed and interwoven with the story of my own special needs—alcoholism and eating disorders.

It should be no surprise to any person of faith that God works through the most broken. As a Christian, I glean examples of this throughout the Bible, from Moses to David to the motley crew of disciples. I wonder if those folks knew how broken they were when God called them to follow him?

A pivotal moment in the story of Adam's Camp came when Adam learned to walk independently for the first time when he is six years old. For me, learning to walk in sobriety came much later. Yet both Adam and I found that learning to walk, both physically and emotionally, was made miraculously complete by leaning into the love and grace of God and others.

"I could walk a mile in your shoes, but I already know they're just as uncomfortable as mine. Let's walk next to each other instead..."

— **Lynda Meyers**

1

The Tennessee Waltz

WHEN I WAS 18 months old, I could sing the entire song, "Tennessee Waltz" on key. My mother made me sit in my little green Naugahyde rocking chair in the living room and sing for our neighbors and relatives. Sometimes I would comply, or if I just wasn't feeling it, refuse, but I knew my mom was so proud of me when I performed.

I didn't understand it at the time, but I believe I learned at an early age to interpret my mother's pride as love. I grew up in the 50s and it wasn't common practice in that era for parents to tell kids how much they were loved. There was great fear that kids would become conceited if they were praised too often. Nobody wanted proud or boastful kids, so the lid was kept on praise and children were left to figure out their value on their own.

Consequently, I allowed others to determine my value by seeking status and praise from them. Usually, my accomplishments and efforts to be a best friend bought me the security I was seeking, but I certainly wasn't above stealing a few things from JC Penny on a "shopping spree" if that's what made me cool in someone's eyes. If smoking corn silk behind the greenhouse in Tommy's backyard was the chosen activity of the evening, I was there if it elevated my status. If instigating the forbidden activity enhanced my status even further as a leader, I was front and center on that also. One minute I was writing the school song for Rosedale Elementary School, and the next drafting the strategy for a group pillage of the neighbor's apple orchard. I think that would be referred to as multi-tasking today.

Don't get me wrong. I am not singing a woe-is-me story about how my mom didn't love me. I think she loved me fiercely, but she lost her mom when she was 12, so her role model for mothering was taken from her early in her life. She made a great go of being my mom, considering the lack of tools she possessed.

Though she did her best to meet the needs of my brother and me, our mom was consumed with my father. My dad was an alcoholic. The kind you would find on the street were it not for someone taking care of him, and that someone was my mom for my dad. My father was a man of great talent with a good career that he washed away with booze in the bars of downtown Denver and in the basement of our house. My dad loved me too, but he basically disappeared behind the bottles hidden all over our house.

Going downstairs to see my dad who watched hours of sports on TV and seeing a bottle of vodka tucked behind his chair let me know exactly where I stood with him at that moment. His speech may have been slurred and I could smell the booze in each word he said. It didn't really matter what he said to me, because the message was always clear: "My bottle of vodka is more important to me than you are. I want you to think you are my priority. I am going to act like you don't know that bottle is behind me and we can both pretend our lives are just fine." I was angry and sad and desperately confused.

I was conflicted about my role in my dad's alcoholism. I wasn't sure if I was supposed to try and fix it or continue to pretend it didn't exist. I hated his drinking, and I hated the fighting it caused between my parents. Each time I found one of his bottles around the house, I would imagine pouring it out in an effort to "save" my dad and restore peace to our family. But I never found the courage to pour out the bottle, and I couldn't save my dad.

In a desperate attempt to wrestle attention from my dad's alcoholism to me I faked an appendicitis attack and actually had my appendix removed when I was nine. That strategy backfired as I don't remember being lonelier in my life than I was those long nights in the hospital My parents came to visit me in the evenings, but the overnights alone proved agonizing. Perhaps I believed my medical crisis would divert my dad's attention from booze long enough to provide me the attention and care I was seeking. But when I returned home after the surgery, nothing had changed. My dad was still drunk, and my mom was still angry and afraid and continued to try and argue him into being sober.

My father's alcoholism was complicated by diabetes, and every year for the last several years of his life, he would go for a week to the VA Hospital to dry out. Those were peaceful times in our house. I didn't always want to go visit my dad, but when I did go, I got to get a milkshake from the hospital canteen. I could hardly wait for that milkshake. Those visits to the sterile, antiseptic halls of the VA Hospital were unsettling and served up a vivid picture of my dad's disease. That cold, creamy milkshake in the conventional tulip shaped glass absorbed every feeling I had about my dad's diseases. I lost myself in the sweet, constantly satisfying joy of that milkshake. I may not have had any control over my dad's alcoholism, but I knew exactly what I was getting when I ordered that ever satisfying, always reliable, comforting milkshake. My memories of those milkshakes are more vivid than my memories of my dad. I find that incredibly sad today.

What memories I do have of my dad are few and far between. Much of the sorrow I carry about him today resides in the empty place memories of the time I had with him should reside. I remember so little about him. My earliest memory is when I would jump out of the coat closet to surprise him when he came home from work. I was probably four or five at the time. I don't know how long that ritual lasted, but I do remember my mom telling me my dad's feelings were hurt when I quit doing it. I don't remember the sound of his voice, the smell of him, or even what he looked like other than what I see in photos.

I believe my dad was a good man when he was sober. He was never abusive, but alcohol robbed me of a relationship with him. It stole most of the time I could have had with him and it erased any memory I had of what good times we did share. Even the things I do remember are not really memories of *him,* but rather memories of things he did. When the trips to Disneyland he promised never materialized, and so many other promises fell by the wayside, I honestly think I quit seeing him. My defense was to distract myself with food or by getting out of the house.

I can't imagine what my daily life would have been like without the neighborhood kids. We lived on a single city block in south Denver which dead ended at Vassar Street on the south and a pig farm on the north. On that one block, there were 38 kids. Our homes were small, but that didn't limit the number of baby boomers born to the families living in them.

Our neighborhood was fairly typical of many middle-class neighborhoods in the 50's and 60's, but to those of us who grew up there, it was an adventure park. Our neighborhood shielded me in many ways from the chaos in my own home as I was usually outside playing or away at other kids houses. In the summer, the lack of air conditioning combined with tight quarters resulted in our being outside every night, organizing games of ditch 'em, building tents on our clotheslines and camping out, riding our bikes, or hitching our wagons to the neighbor's riding lawn mower to parade around the block.

In the winter, my friend Janet and I would create shows. We would lip sync and dance to the latest songs on the hit parade, and all the neighbors and my aunts would attend. It seemed like we spent months preparing our acts, making and sending invitations, decorating the basement with crepe paper and baking refreshments, but I'm sure it wasn't more than a few weeks. Since my chubby body served as evidence of my love for comfort food, I'm sure me dancing around Janet in a yellow swimsuit clutching a pink chiffon shawl and a wand and syncing Mr. Sandman was quite the vision.

There were some lovely families living on our block but my most vivid memories center around the others, the crazy people whose antics lit up the night sky with police lights and sirens, or others who lived lives contrary to what you would imagine given their professions. These are the families that made me feel like my life was a normal one.

Take Ethel, for example. She was a nurse who lived across the street with her husband and two adopted boys. Though Ethel was a nurse at the local hospital, she lived in a home overrun with cat hair and filth. Her son, my friend and contemporary, was highly allergic to cats, but this didn't keep Ethel from having three of them. Margie was a single mom who had six kids, each from a different father. Margie laid in the backyard with a carefully crafted "M" in masking tape on her back to create a tan featuring her initial. She worked nights at a bar. She would chase her kids down the street with a razor strap with which she beat them well and often. More than once, the police arrived at Margie's house in the middle of the night to haul away the latest drunk she had taken in. In today's world, she would certainly have lost those kids and spent much of her life in prison for child abuse. To us, it was just another day on South Washington Street. These bizarre circumstances made my life seem blessed in comparison, so my ability to acknowledge my need for stability in our own home was pushed further into a state of denial. I created my own reality.

In many ways, it sounds like I had a happy and normal childhood. In many ways, I did. But my world was all dreaming and make believe. I imagined the life I wanted through play, and I used that play to craft an illusion – that our family life, where most days were filled with fighting and fear and tiptoeing around my dad, was normal. I continued to nurture the belief that attention was love, and food was happiness. It seemed what happy times there were in our house centered around food...going to the grocery store together and getting to buy a Daffy Apple, making popcorn to eat while we watched Hit Parade, holiday dinners and the occasional meal out. It helped me downplay the constant fighting and my mom begging my father to quit drinking.

On more than one occasion, I woke in the middle of the night to hear my mother tearfully pleading with my dad to drink orange juice to mitigate diabetic shock. Instead, he would be standing at the kitchen sink, drinking whiskey. I believe he was resorting to his basic instinct to drink during these episodes that seemed to go on forever. Tears soaked my pillow as I silently begged my father to STOP. My stomach filled with fear and what I can only describe as agony as I laid there, helpless. I was sure my dad was going to die during those heartbreaking fights, with me lying just a few feet away in my lavender bedroom.

I don't remember ever talking with my mom or dad about these episodes the next day. We continued pretending. More food meant less feeling. I think my mom and brother also bought the lie that there was nothing a good snack couldn't fix. We were desperate for normalcy, and we- at least I- believed we had created it through food. Fond memories of my dad often centered around food. He was from Missouri, and he could put a good southern breakfast on the table with the best of them. Scrambled eggs, bacon, fried potatoes and homemade biscuits and gravy were his specialty. Sometimes, we had this for dinner on Friday nights as well. We operated like a normal family around the kitchen table when my dad was present during times he was at least reasonably sober. Food became the great healer.

I was always chubby, but I grew heavier and heavier into my elementary school years. When I felt lonely or discontent, it was natural for me to believe I was unhappy because I was fat. Kids teased me. My knick name became Karel the Barrel. Every year we had field day at school, and I was always the last one chosen for teams and certainly the last to cross the finish line in the one-hundred-yard dash. I laid awake the entire night every year before that day. I was mortified by my lack of athletic talent.

I hated the way I looked, and I became boy crazy at a very young age, so my weight didn't help in my quest to find my first boyfriend. When I was sad or anxious or afraid, it was easy for me to blame my excess weight instead of acknowledging the dysfunction within my family. That would have been far more painful, so I just continued to eat. We snacked constantly at home in front of the TV. Right after dinner, the bag of chips or candy came out to compliment the ice cream and cookies we had had for dessert. I always snacked between meals, and there was always an abundance of sugary drinks at our disposal. I could hardly wait for the popsicle man to drive by every summer day so I could add to my sugar intake.

When we were in our pre-teens, my friend Timmy (not his real name) across the street and I use to put together feasts to share in the afternoons while his mother was at work. We would make peanut butter and jelly sandwiches, chips, ice cream, cookies, crackers, and anything else we could conjure up. Honestly, these were full-on binges. He used food in the same way I did, and we became fast, chubby friends.

I spent my childhood developing pretty lousy eating habits that may not have been great at nourishing my body, but certainly seemed to be filling something more than my stomach. Food took the edge off the ragged contours of my wounded soul.

When I was in 6th grade, I was pulled out of class to attend a small group session for kids who were overweight. When I returned to class, my teacher, no Twiggy herself, looked at me with pity and announced to the class that there was "nothing wrong with being pleasingly plump." This was definitely not the kind of attention I was seeking. I was completely paralyzed by embarrassment. I could feel the tears welling and my heart racing as every eye in the class turned to assess my size. Her comment reinforced my belief that I *was* my weight. I was fat and ugly and unlovable. I was on the outside looking in at the perfect lives of all the skinny kids.

While food comforted me in the moment, it led to the weight gain that fueled my need for comfort. Essentially, I was feeding the very demon that had been impersonating as my solution for my entire life. I had to find a way to mitigate the weight gain and control my reliance on food. Self-control became my goal. I was going to wrestle this demon to the ground.

2

If It's to Be, It's Up to Me

THE SUMMER FOLLOWING sixth grade I made the first major decision to change my life. After my dad's many promises of Disneyland and happier times failed to materialize, and my father's alcoholism progressed, I became more and more convinced I needed to take charge of my life – and probably the lives of others.

I asked my mom to take me to the doctor to get diet pills so that I could lose weight and live happily ever after. Since I was convinced the hollow place growing inside me was a result of being fat, this effort to get my weight under control was also an attempt to find the sense of security I was unknowingly seeking. She complied, as did my doctor, and I began a dance with diet pills that lasted well into my college years.

I thought, by using diet pills to increase my metabolism and decrease my appetite, I was winning the battle against food. Pushing my desire to eat into a corner made me feel victorious and powerful. I had no idea what I was dealing with. It certainly wasn't the food and it wasn't my weight. I was trying to suppress the very substance that provided my comfort. My chaos (which I had grown quite comfortable with in my home), was my best friend and my worst enemy. I thought I had gained control of food and eating, but what I actually think I did was just piss it off.

Showing up to junior high that fall twenty pounds lighter did cause quite a stir. Karel the Barrel now gained attention for her weight loss rather than her size. Now that I was skinny and pretty, I was sure all my problems were solved. I could finally get the boy and be accepted like the other girls, and my belief that skinny equaled happy meant I now could live a perfect life like I believed most of the other kids did.

While continuing my quest to be noticed and popular by achieving, I also got tangled up with a few kids who found their way into the justice system by stealing cars, theft, and various misdemeanors. There was more than one way to get attention, and I was willing to push the boundaries with the legal system to gain the attention of a particularly charming boy who had a tendency to break the law. One night, when I was about 14, my boyfriend came very close to talking me into joining them in stealing a car to take for a joy ride. I would have had to sneak out of my house at night (something I had done before) to be a part of this adventure, and somehow I made the decision to stay home. My boyfriend and his brother were caught and began a relationship with the law that lasted well into adulthood. I somehow managed to move out of that circle of friends, but I know that I gave my parents a run for their money throughout those years. The burden of reining me in fell to my mom as my dad continued to deteriorate. He had lost his job as a CPA and was unable to stay sober for any length of time.

My father died when I was 15 and in the ninth grade. The day he died, I went to school so I could attend a district-wide student council meeting, but also to gain the attention of my peers. It wasn't comfort I was seeking. It was attention. Being the center of attention on the day my father died made me feel wanted and loved and important. Rather than being surrounded by my family and providing comfort to my mom, I wanted to be with my friends. On a day when grief would seem most natural., I felt relief. The constant tension in our small home surrounding my dad's drinking had been silenced. Our day-to-day problems no longer included finding empty bottles behind the couch or listening to the constant bickering caused by my father's horrible disease and my mother's misguided attempts to "fix" him.

The following year, I started South High School which had a student body pushing 2400 students. It was the perfect challenge for my continued quest for popularity. One of the first things I did in the fall of my sophomore year was to run for student council representative, which I won. I found I gained the most respect and attention when I held positions of prominence. I didn't have to work as hard for the attention I sought when people looked up to me. I loved the competition and pageantry and vibrance of South. I made friends easily, and I loved all the tension and drama surrounding anything to do with school activities and boys.

In addition to belonging to every club and running for office at school, I also had an insatiable desire to be loved by boys. Today, I know that the many wonderful guys I dated were really more prey to me than partner. As soon as I had established someone as my official boyfriend, I lost interest and moved on to the next victim. The amount of time I spent in each relationship was directly proportional to the amount of time it took me to get them to love me.

I think that pattern reflected my true self esteem at the time. I didn't want to be with someone who would want to be with me. The accolades surrounding me did not reflect the soul sickness inside me. I had no idea.

Glory was my survival in those years, and it was continually reinforced by my success. I worked hard to find my way into the spotlight and was rewarded by being elected cheerleader, prom queen, and many other outward achievements.

Without this attention and these accolades, I felt invisible. I had no idea what inherent value was; I believed my worth *was* what I did. I enjoyed the things I participated in, but all those titles, activities and accomplishments became the vessel that held my self-worth.

As a senior, I finally landed the guy I had been stalking for months, and I believed that life could not get any better. My best friend Wendy, who was elected Senior Prom Queen (a scenario we had dreamed of as sophomores), had landed the boy of her dreams as well.

High school is filled with wonderful memories. We went skating on the lake at Washington Park and attended all the football and basketball games.

The biggest risk takers among us (that would include me) would sneak onto the school athletic fields at night and jump in the foam contraptions used by the track team to train in the springtime. In the winter, we engaged in the horribly dangerous act of tying a rope to the back of a car and "shoe skiing". Tee-peeing houses was always fun, but we decided to take it to the next level by stealing road construction signs and putting them in the yards of the tee-peed houses as an added feature. A highlight of our shenanigans was the night I drove my car across the grass in Washington Park to catch up with a carload of boys we were chasing. I'm pretty sure jail would have been involved in much of what we did these days, but in those days, it was chalked up to youthful pranks.

I continued the battle with my weight. I was on and off diet pills all through high school, and I remember skipping lunch many days in an effort to lose weight. I always wanted to be skinnier, no matter what I weighed which was well within normal during those years.

In spite of my continued struggles, my school days were filled with joy. I will be forever grateful for that special time in my life and all that it taught me. I felt invincible when I graduated in 1967.

What I didn't realize until later was that I had spent 18 years of my life building a platform of awards, status and friends who held my self-worth, security and sanity aloft on a pillar of sand.

3

Gifts

WHILE MY MOTIVES may have been those of a selfish opportunist at times, the truth is I really loved doing the things I became involved with. I gravitated toward anything that required organizing and motivating people toward a common goal. Whether it was our annual Goodwill Drive which resulted in a parking lot lined with tall paper bags filled with donations from the community or the next big dance before which I could often be found teetering on a ten foot ladder hanging crepe paper, I often found myself at the helm.

There was a contest when I was in sixth grade for our church Vacation Bible School to see who could bring the most friends for the week. The prize was the honor of being Queen or King for a Day with our adorable youth leader, Russ. Motivated by my crush on Russ, I managed to recruit so many kids to attend the church had to send a bus to our neighborhood to pick them all up.

I was very proud of the leadership positions in which I found myself. I used my leadership to prove my significance. I had no idea my leadership ability was a gift. It is not something for which I had to strive--leadership has always come naturally to me. I have been blessed with the type of mind that formulates solutions and the type of passion that inspires others to collaborate. I am grateful to have been given these gifts. They have opened many doors for me, allowing me to enjoy some incredible experiences, and to meet some remarkable people. It took me some time to learn to use my leadership as a tool to serve others rather than a talent to lord over them.

Regardless of my motivation, the activities and situations in which I found myself throughout my school days certainly helped me refine and develop my gifts

Another gift I was given was compassion for the underdog. We lived near the Colorado State Home for Children. This orphanage took in the unwanted kids from the poorest and least equipped families in the state. It was a cold and soulless facility, and those kids who so longed for love and acceptance attended the same schools I attended. Today, many of these kids would be identified as having special needs, but in the 50s and 60s, they were referred to as mentally retarded.

A waif of a girl named Dora who lived at the home captured my heart when I first met her. She was shy and had a smell about her I can only describe as musty. I showed her kindness, and she immediately clung to me. I didn't realize at the time how starved these kids were for someone to love them, and Dora's demands were more than I was prepared for. So while I often found myself trying to avoid Dora, I still felt the tug of compassion for her.

Shirley, another resident of the Children's Home, was the polar opposite of Dora. She was tough and loud and let us all know that she was not to be messed with. But I saw through her tough exterior, and like Dora, she wanted to become my constant companion. I will never forget walking home from junior high one day, seeing Shirley charging across the field from the home to envelop me in her formidable arms. I was pretty sure I was in over my head.

In high school, it was Pat who captured my heart. He was a kid with multiple deformities who wanted more than anything to belong. His small stature and awkward gait set him up for some pretty unacceptable abuse from many of the guys he tried to be friends with, and I often found myself coming to his defense.

Looking back, I could have done much more to protect and advocate for these kids, but I was unequipped to offer these kids what they needed at my age as I juggled my own needs for love and acceptance.

My love for writing has served me well throughout my life. A little added bonus to that is my aptitude for rhyming just about anything. It is a relatively useless gift, but when a good poem is called for, I'm your girl. I write poems for tributes, birthdays, and roasts. It's fun.

Another gift that has served me well is the ability to use language as a speaker. Speaking in front of others comes naturally for me and I can usually organize thoughts and articulate them effectively. Again, this has always been true for me, so I certainly view it as a gift. I did work hard on my speech for the High School State Sojourner's Speech competition, and my writing and delivery allowed me to represent South in the finals of that competition. My Job's Daughter days offered many opportunities for public speaking, as did my campaigns for student government office. I loved an audience, so my gift for speaking continued to reinforce my belief that more people hearing me equaled more people loving me so that I could love myself. When I considered these gifts talents, I used them to bolster my and your opinion of me. The truth was, external validation only created a temporary high that lasted only as long as the attention did. Inside, I still felt emptiness.

When operating from a place of pride, self-loathing over gifts one doesn't have is just as powerful as the false bravado created by achievements. I was jealous of gifts others had that I didn't, such as athleticism.

Gym class was a nightmare for me. I dreaded that sleepless night before field day because everyone had to participate in every event, and I could always count on being last in the fifty-yard dash. Pure humiliation. My only ribbon came in the shoe kick, which was poor compensation for the public display of ineptitude I exhibited on the track. I couldn't ski, and I sucked pretty much every sport I tried.

I love singing and dancing and am good enough at both, but never good enough to stand out. I was in the choir, but not the soloist. I relished my role with the Senior Dance Line and as a cheerleader, but I certainly would never have been considered a great dancer. Participating in these activities taught me how to be a "part of" which was valuable to a girl who was always striving to be at the top of the heap.

I think it is hard to understand the true nature of gifts without having an appreciation of the giver. I believed in a God who was there to be my pinch hitter, not the one who had created me in His image. My skills fill me with pride. I believed my skills were something I had created. It became easy to use my talents to continue to glorify myself.

I did not view my skills as gifts and sure didn't credit God for any of my successes. That would have required me to relinquish belief in my complete control of my life, present, past and future. My need for that control was as strong as my need for the next breath. When my parents, because of their own woundedness, proved emotionally unreliable, I took the reins of my life, pushed emotions and feelings aside, and charged into the future waving a flag of independence and self-determination. I held onto those reins until my hands bled and I controlled myself into a rigid prison that was the epitome of powerlessness.

Throughout my childhood and teens, God wove His way in and out of my life. Every weekend included Sundays at Bonnie Brae Baptist Church. We always attended Sunday School followed by the church service. I followed the bible story characters across the felt board our teachers used to teach us about the Bible and learned my favorite hymns from the Baptist hymnal. We followed the rules of our religion.

I viewed God as a good guy who was watching over us to make sure we didn't get out of line. I prayed for the things I wanted and tried to make sure I was doing enough good to earn them. Unfortunately, our family didn't get the grace part of faith. It wasn't five minutes after pulling away from the curb leaving church before my mom was criticizing something someone had worn or done at church that day. My mom's insecurities made her vulnerable to gossip, and she perpetuated it with the best of them. God was for Sundays, but aside from rote prayers before going to bed or before dinner, He didn't make an appearance in our daily lives very often.

While I had been taught God is all powerful, I had no idea I was made to have a relationship with Him. I didn't understand the incred-ible message of love and hope He imparted by sending Jesus to model and facilitate that relationship. I thought God sent Jesus because he was angry with us and needed a way to let us into Heaven, but I have since learned he loved us desperately and sent Jesus to show us the extent of His love and the depth of His desire to be a living, breathing part of our lives. I didn't get that His unconditional love was all I really needed, so my woundedness and pride continued to drive me further toward self-reliance and away from God.

4

Honors to Addiction

I SHOULD HAVE known when I pulled up to my dorm at the University of Northern Colorado that my trajectory to popularity may be challenged at this stage of the game. To begin with, it was clearly a much larger stage. Secondly, the air smelled like something I can only describe as cow manure and burnt mashed potatoes.

Greeley was a town surrounded by cattle and sugar beet process-ing plants. I equate it to what was to become my college experience in that, no matter how hard I tried, the environment I was living in was permeated with the smell of my woundedness. Without the hon-ors and accolades that held me up at home, I felt lonely and empty. Without others to tell me who I was, I was invisible.

I know most kids feel homesick and many experience loneliness when they first go to college. For me, the solution was to escape those feelings as quickly as possible. Rather than using this as a time to ex-plore and make peace with my authentic self , I reverted to what I thought had worked for me my entire life. I needed to establish my status on campus. Dorm life provided few opportunities for this type of hierarchy, but I do remember seeking out friendships with those girls I thought would be most popular. The party scene was on, and I was the first to jump at the chance to be the life of the party. Not once did I think that it might not be a good idea for me to drink. I didn't really like beer, but I drank plenty of it. I also learned to enjoy cigarettes, another habit my dad possessed that I swore would never become a part of my life.

When sorority rush rolled around, I determined that Delta Zeta Sorority was a perfect fit for me. It was arguably the sorority comprised of the most popular girls on campus and had the reputation of being big on the party. Not all my sorority sisters partied like I did, but I gravitated toward the ones who did. One of my proudest moments came my sophomore year when I represented DZ in a beer drinking contest at the Library, the popular FAC (Friday Afternoon Club) with students on campus. I not only out-chugged all my fellow sorority challengers, but in a dramatic faceoff, out-chugged the fraternity champion as well. My mother was not impressed when she found *that* plaque in my bedroom drawer. I, on the other hand, couldn't have been prouder. For me, there was no such thing as bad publicity when it came to making me stand out.

Wendy, my best friend from high school, transferred to UNC our sophomore year after completing her freshman year in a small school in Oklahoma. She and I attempted to relive the glory of our high school cheerleading days by trying out for Pom Pom girl. We both were selected, but the experience was different than what we had enjoyed in high school. We really weren't that big a deal to most people.

Wendy and I were roommates in a rambling yellow wood-shingled-house we shared with six other girls. Big Yellow, as it was known, sat on a prominent corner on campus and became a known entity among our classmates, especially the guys. I had hoped my identity as a Pom-pom Girl, a Delta Zeta and our house full of girls would boost my reputation and self-esteem. I didn't have the number of suitors I had in High school, so my popularity with the guys was not feeding my ego. I was not standing out. In reality, I had plenty of friends, my grades were fine, and my life was good. But inside, my insatiable need for praise and attention was not being fed. Enter more alcohol, more cigarettes and more food.

It's not easy to maintain a healthy weight while eating on a tight budget, drinking excessively, and using sugar to fuel late night study sessions. Walking to classes on a large campus and practicing dance routines with the Poms wasn't enough to offset the amount of eating and drinking I was doing. I felt lonely and invisible without the shroud of accomplishments that made me stand out all through high school. The more lost I felt, the more I ate and drank to anesthetize those feelings. The more weight I gained, the worse I felt about myself. The hole inside I had disguised with external success was growing bigger, and I was desperate to control those aching feelings. I didn't want to keep gaining weight, and the diet pills were no longer working, so I entered into a whole new world of self-deceit and perceived control.

I had to find a way to not gain weight. The harder I tried to diet, the more out of control I felt. That desperate need to control my weight led me to discover what seemed the perfect solution-binging and purging. I don't remember the first time I threw up, but I do remember it took a long time and was really difficult. When I drank, my bulimia (which was an unnamed disorder at the time) was at its worst. I know now I was looking for ways to manage my loneliness and feelings of inadequacy as I fought for control of my life. I was still on and off diet pills but drinking the way I did, eating donuts for breakfast and binging in the evenings led to a steady weight gain. There were many nights, after tying one on, that I would come home and eat half a cake or other food that was in the refrigerator that was meant for all of us before throwing it all up and stumbling off to bed. It wasn't long before my roommates identified me as the culprit.

Sometimes, I would go days watching what I ate, only to completely lose control under the influence of alcohol. In high school my weight fluctuation was dictated by diet pills and will power. Once I started drinking, my will power became non-existent and I engaged in binges during which I consumed ridiculous amounts of food. Though throwing up was difficult for me at first, it eventually became easier which made my binges more frequent.

Wendy and I were not nearly as close as we were in high school. She didn't like smoking (which I and most of my roommates did). After realizing the party life wasn't for her, she dropped out of my sorority just weeks after joining. She went home a lot on weekends. My comings and goings at all hours disrupted her sleep and serenity. She didn't drink like I did and took the concept of actually being in school more seriously than I did. About the only thing we still shared aside from our Pom Pom Girl life was our love for kids. We were both elementary education majors.

Ever since I fell in love with my third-grade teacher, Miss Lillge, I had wanted to be a teacher. That passion never wavered. My natural love for kids was always a part of my life as a teenager when I babysat often and volunteered in a preschool as a part of my high school curriculum. The honest, unfiltered view of the world and its people that kids have fed my soul.

You would think my desire to be a teacher would have inspired me to work hard toward my goals in college. Because of my love of writing, I was also an English major which proved to require much more attention than I was willing to allot to academics. My priority to stand out socially over succeeding with my studies was never more evident than during my sophomore year when I was nominated by my sorority for Miss UNC. My goals for that quarter were to lose weight, put together a song and dance routine, and find the appropriate swimsuit, costume, and evening gown for the pageant. The idea of being on stage, the center of attention, vying for a title that would finally declare me not only visible, but *the* most visible girl on campus filled me with visions of grandeur. Finally, I would obtain the title and recognition I had been lacking and the hole inside me would be filled at last. I had a goal to maintain my weight for the chance to receive yet another crown. I don't think I made it onto academic probation that quarter, but I was close.

I sang and danced my heart out for the talent portion of the contest, channeling my best Barbara Streisand on a song from the musical Funny Girl. My interview went perfectly. I had lost some weight by spending evenings at a health club and cutting back on the donuts. I practiced my routine several times a day rather than studying. In the dramatic finale, I was first runner up to a beautiful girl whose talent was sewing her own dress. Sewing her own dress???? Clearly, unparalleled beauty won out again, and just like that, the pageant was over. I had done well, but all I really had to show for this was a quarter in which my grades plummeted and my internal struggle, no longer distracted the by promise of fame and attention, returned.

After that spring quarter, Janet, a friend from both high school and college and I decided an adventure was in order. Taking risks was never a problem for me, so when the opportunity to go to South Lake Tahoe to work for the summer arose, I was in. I remember it took some talking to convince my mom that jumping on a plane with no job, no place to live, and no money was a good idea for a couple of 20-year-old girls, but as usual I had my way.

When we arrived in Lake Tahoe, we found a cheap hotel for the first night of close calls. The proprietor was drunk and insistent as he tried to push his way into our room late that night. Fortunately, he was too drunk to push his way past two strong and freaked-out girls. The next day we scanned the classifieds and found a house to share with six other girls who had been recruited as Blackjack dealers, all from the University of Oklahoma. Since we weren't 21, Janet and I had to find jobs in the less glamorous sectors of the tourist industry. She found a job as a hotel maid and I landed a counter job at the Tahoe Burger Bar. Just the place for a girl with an eating disorder who has just come off a three-month diet.

Predictably, I again felt lonely and invisible in a new environment where I knew no one but my friend. The problem of transportation to work was solved by hitchhiking to and from the Tahoe Burger Bar every day. More than once I accepted rides with men who drove out of their way with the hopes of giving me more than a ride home, but by the grace of God, I was always able to talk my way out of any assault. I went to the casinos with my fake ID where I drank and gambled, but I found the glitz and glamour depressing. I could see the desperation and despair of the compulsive gamblers and found the environment hollow and even more lonely. Plenty of burgers, beer and binges pushed me to new heights with my weight, and my quest for adventure and love did nothing to fill the void. I had been dating a guy named Mike that year who flew out to see me, which even then seemed like compensation for not finding romance in Tahoe. What should have been a great adventure only magnified my emptiness, and no amount of alcohol or food could mitigate my loneliness.

5

Desperate Defense

BY THE TIME I moved from the dorm to the sorority house junior year, I had the good sense to pick a roommate who had a lifestyle similar to mine. Karen was a free-spirited girl who said what she thought and lived her life outside the accepted norms for 1970 when sex outside of marriage was frowned upon. Karen drank with abandon, and she chose a boyfriend who beat her regularly. She came from an abusive, alcoholic family, so she was living out what she knew. She was hilarious, and our irreverence for the mundane gave us great fodder for gossip late into many nights. We were both major slobs — our room was covered with clothes that belonged in our empty closet and dirty dishes that belonged in the kitchen. I think our room was an outward expression of an inward battle within each of us.

I continued my Pom Pom girl activities and was active with the sorority. Still seeking fame and adoration, I jumped at the chance to become a lounge singer. I auditioned with a small combo led by my Generative Transformational Grammar (I know – and it was as hideous a class as it sounds) teacher, and he brought me into the small group of musicians who landed gigs around town in the few bars that had live music. I would pound down a few scotch-and-sodas before getting on stage to belt my heart out to the latest Carole King hit of the day, or to the sultry sounds of classic lounge tunes like, "When Sunny Gets

Blue" or "Cry Me a River". I honestly have no idea if I was any good or not, because I was usually just drunk enough to *think* I was fantastic. The response from the six disinterested people in the audience at the Greeley Ramada Inn didn't really give me enough to go on.

Junior year was the year of the passing for my pledge class. A passing is a ceremony in which a candle adorned with flowers is passed around the circle of girls in our sorority while we all sing the sorority theme song until it is blown out by the lucky girl who has just gotten either pinned or engaged. This was her way of announcing that she was committed to THE ONE. The candle was delivered to the house by the florist earlier in the day, so the anticipation around who the lucky girl was ensured a full house for the ceremony. Marriage was the natural next step after graduation in those days, so many college sweethearts became engaged senior year and tied the knot after getting their degree. I suspect the desire to be a part of this dramatic ceremony was a major reason I became pinned to Mike.

I continued to date Mike through my junior year but was never convinced that he was THE ONE. He was kind and well-liked. He was president of his fraternity the previous year. Our personalities and communications styles were different from each other. I suspect part of what held us together was our love for booze. He wanted to get married, but I was still unconvinced that Mike was my life partner.

In the spring of that year, Mike was student teaching in another town when I ran for president of Delta Zeta. In a very close election, I lost. My need for love and significance was demonstrated in living color when I lost that election. After the results were announced, I walked down the street to a pay phone, called Mike, and told him that I would marry him. I had to do something to make myself matter, and marrying Mike seemed the most logical way to matter after being rejected by my sorority sisters. Suddenly, I had no identity.

I had my passing at the sorority the next week and spent the remainder of the spring and the beginning of the summer planning my wedding. Once again, I had purpose. Mike and I were married in August of 1970 after my junior year in my family church. We found a nice basement apartment next to a sorority sister and her new husband and began our life together. Mike had graduated and landed a job teaching in Longmont while I was finishing my coursework in preparation to student teach in the spring of my senior year. Nothing much changed after we were married; we continued to party with friends like we always had.

Erie Elementary was my placement for student teaching, and I loved my supervising teacher, the staff and most of all the kids. Teaching second grade was challenging and fun for me, and after I completed that quarter, I was offered a job for the following year. You would think that working in an elementary school would limit my opportunities to drink, but that couldn't be further from the truth at Erie Elementary. After school on Fridays, many of the teachers would go to a bar down the road and get completely hammered. Those of us who were hard core would go from that bar to others and often not return home until after midnight. Sometimes Mike joined us and sometimes he didn't. Incredibly, we were all driving drunk at a time when DUIs were few and far between. The number of teachers who had affairs with other teachers and the principal was legendary.

Mike had also connected with the drinkers in his school, so there was always a party on the weekends. We moved to a roomy garden level apartment in Longmont when I began student teaching which brought us both closer to our jobs. I began trying my hand at domesticity – cooking, sewing, creating a home. My interest in sewing was short lived, but my love/hate relationship with food inspired me to become a pretty good cook. My pattern of drinking one beer a night during the week followed by excessive drinking and binging on the weekends was well established by then, so I continued to struggle with unwelcome weight gain.

In yet another effort to lose weight, I decided to try weight watchers. This was actually a pivotal move for me in my battle with food. When presented a plan that was less about deprivation and more about healthy eating, I began to practice meal planning and eating that was not only satisfying but was sustainable as well. I began to follow a pattern that included three meals a day and very little snacking which was contrary to how I had always eaten. I stayed with this long enough to lose the extra weight and more importantly, to permanently change my eating habits. Between this new way of eating during the week and my completely crazy binge-purge behavior on the weekends, I managed to maintain an acceptable weight.

We entertained a lot, mostly to ensure there was always an excuse to drink ourselves silly. It seemed like a perfectly normal life to me, and for some of those folks, I'm sure it was typical for their mid-twenties. I thought everyone we partied with woke up the next day with a hangover (which many did) and an empty hole inside (which most of them didn't). I was pretty sure I was the only one binging and purging throughout the party.

I would dive into the appetizers the minute I walked in the door (or if the party was at our house, the minute anyone else walked in the door) and would wash them down with a beer, or a scotch, or a margarita or a glass of wine or whatever drink was being offered. The source of the alcohol was far less important to me than the effect of the alcohol. I would always start moderately like everyone else, but the more I drank, the more I ate. If it was a dinner party, I would usually throw up between the cocktail hour and the main course so I would have plenty of room to eat more. By dessert, I would usually make myself available in the kitchen so I could continue to sneak leftover food and sample the dessert while helping serve it. I had no "off switch" for either food or alcohol by that time in the evening. When others switched to water and were finished with dinner, I would continue to drink and snack on whatever was still laying around after throwing up my dinner. It was as if I was making up for the week of deprivation I had imposed on myself Monday through Friday. I believed I had earned the right to binge and purge because of the excellent control I often exhibited regarding the amount I ate and drank during the week. Since my weight remained fairly stable using this rather bizarre method of weight management, I thought it was the perfect way to be in complete control. I had no idea that during those early days of my marriage, I was establishing a pattern that would imprison me for many years to come.

Mike and I became good friends with Fred and Elaine, a woman I taught with and her husband who lived in Boulder. They were both CU graduates and big fans of CU football. We would meet at their house for Bloody Marys around 11 and have lunch, go to the game and drink throughout, then party at someone's house or in town afterward. Those games constituted about twelve solid hours of drinking, and we all managed to stay conscious. It wasn't unusual for us to go to happy hour on Friday and a game on Saturday.

I wanted to continue to sing after we left Greeley, so I connected with a folksinger at the Wine Cellar, a bar in Longmont. Sometimes, after a full day of drinking at a CU game, I would go to sing with him. Again, I was inebriated enough to feel incredibly talented and may or may not have been a complement to the show. I would get home after two a.m. from those stints.

After about a year of marriage, it was clear that Mike and I had problems. It was becoming painfully obvious that the only time we really connected was when we were drinking. Of course, being married to Mike – or I suspect anyone else- did not bring me the relief or security I sought. I struggled to make conversation with Mike and our intimacy had vanished. I moved out after about 18 months together.

A fellow teacher and friend and I got an apartment in Northglenn, a town on the northern outskirts of Denver. Though I was still very much married, I used the separation as permission to drink and flirt and continue my search for the perfect man who would fill the emptiness inside my sole. This was a painfully low point in my life as I was incredibly careless with my life and with Mike's feelings. Selfish and self-centered described me to a tee. During our separation, I met a drummer in the band of one of the bars I frequented. He was a tall, dark, dashing guy who treated me poorly, which meshed well with my self-image at that point. Mike came to our apartment late one night to talk to me about reconciling, and my roommate had to tell him I was out. I felt badly for Mike and my roommate, but not badly enough to change my behavior. I wanted to be happy, and believed I deserved that at all cost. Mike and I divorced after two years of marriage, but instead of the liberation I was seeking, the hole inside just got bigger. There didn't seem to be enough booze, food or men to fill it.

6

The Next Victim

MY PARTYING CONTINUED after Mike and I divorced, and I spent many nights in bars looking for Mr. Right. With no online dating available in 1973, there were few opportunities for me to meet single men as an elementary school teacher. I dated a few guys. One of them showered me with gifts and elaborate dates, which I was perfectly willing to accept even though I only viewed him as a friend. I was honest with him about my feelings, but I know he held out hope that his lavish pursuit would one day win me over. I'm sure he was hurt by my continued rejection of him as a lover and boyfriend, and I am not proud that I continued to date him to enjoy the gifts and experiences he so willingly provided. Our relationship held together by our love for alcohol.

I usually visited my mom about once a week. She still lived in the house I grew up in, and life got more interesting in our old neighborhood when a houseful of guys my age moved in next door to her. She had become friendly with one in particular - the guy who actually owned the house. Mom was anxious for me to meet him, but my interest came to a screeching halt when she told me his name was Bob Horney. I should interject here that my maiden name was Wright, my first married name was Keister, and the thought of moving toward the name Horney was definitely not the trajectory I was looking for. Bob Horney? Not doing it for me. But my mom was not to be denied as she practically drug me into our backyard to introduce me to Bob one summer afternoon over our white picket fence.

Bob was good looking enough, but I was annoyed at my mom's insistence and told Bob as much after we were introduced. I believe that my exact words were: "My mom has been *dying* for me to meet you," to which he replied "Nsh to meet you." Huh? It turns out his jaw was wired shut due to an accident playing softball. Our brief and unceremonial introduction resulted in our not speaking again for about six months.

By the time Thanksgiving rolled around that year, Bob's sister Mary Louise and her husband John were living with him while John completed his residency in radiology at CU Medical Center. Bob and his sister had no family in town, so Mom invited them for Thanksgiving dinner. Bob and I had shared a few friendly conversations in the driveway since our initial meeting, and I loved his sister, so it seemed a fun way to spend the holiday. Something clicked between Bob and me that day, and the following day we went downtown to Larimer Square to Christmas shop and have dinner. After a few fits and starts, we began dating.

In spite of my distancing from God, He had not distanced Himself from me. God has a funny way of forcing the issue if He has a plan. In June of that year, Bob was offered a job in New York he had decided to take, and he invited me to come along. In 1975, teaching jobs were few and far between, and I was less than interested in going somewhere I had never been to play house with Bob Horney. The answer to that request was no. A few days later, he took me to a romantic restaurant the overlooked the Denver skyline and proposed. He had a terrible cold, so while his intentions were lovely, I wouldn't say the evening was filled with magic and romance. While I was touched by his proposal, I wasn't that far removed from my divorce and was not feeling swept off my feet. We had great communication and so much fun together, but I wanted my next marriage to be my last, and I wasn't completely sure.

It made perfect sense to me to get together with two of my friends and drinking buddies, get loaded, and *then* decide whether to marry Bob or stay with my teaching job and life in Denver. After a long afternoon of drinking and discussing the pros and cons of this union, we all decided that Bob was a great catch and that I should take the plunge. Fueled by liquid courage, I called him at work and said YES.

A few days and a clear head later, my hesitancy returned. I walked from my mom's house to Bob's to tell him that I didn't think I was ready to marry him and move so far away from the only home I had ever known. I had already quit my job in anticipation of the move to Connecticut, a bedroom community to New York, so after telling Bob the engagement was off, I went back to my mom's to call my school principal and ask if I could return to my job. He agreed to reinstate me, but suggested my resigning, then changing my mind would not be viewed favorably on my record. Hmmm. After giving short consideration to a blemish on my teaching record, I walked back to Bob's and told him I would marry him after all. And *that* is the firm bedrock upon which our marriage began

Bob was to begin his job in New York the following week. He listed his house, took my car as he decided to sell his Datsun 280Z which was sputtering at 100,000 miles, and left me to sell his car and plan the wedding, which we'd decided would be in August. I had two months to check through this list.

As challenging as this was, I did sell his car, and planned the small wedding we would have on August 8th in an open field on beautiful Genesee Mountain in the foothills just outside Denver. We were into 70s culture, and my hippie dress, wildflower bouquet and a flautist in an open field created just the ambiance we were looking for. After a brunch at nearby Hiwan Country Club and a small reception in the yard of a friend's house, Bob and I took off to Connecticut to set up house in a quaint cottage Bob had found in Westport. Looking back, I remember we were both hungover for the wedding, and I was totally wasted on our wedding night.

Although I anticipated missing my friends and family, I was completely unprepared for the dark spiral I fell into over the next four years. As I feared, I was unable to get a teaching job right away, so I applied as a substitute. We lived in a town of old money and insulated families where newcomers were treated politely but were certainly not welcome into the lives of those who had lived there for generations. Our house was at the end of Saviano Lane, and we loved that little house on the creek, but it could not have been more distant from potential friends.

Bob had long commutes to his job in both New York and New Jersey. He was paying his dues and was on the path to success. Bob's Midwest background prepared him with a strong work ethic and a way with people that helped him always succeed at the jobs he had. This one was demanding, and in addition to that he was completing his stint with the National Guard which took him away from home one weekend a month.

I worked on the house and taught a few days a week. I was worried about gaining weight out of boredom, so I found myself taking my structured eating routine to a whole new level. For breakfast, I would have either a small bowl of cereal or a poached egg on ½ an English Muffin. For lunch, thin sliced bread with one still thinner slice of turkey and some carrots and celery. For dinner, I would eat small portions of protein and vegetables followed by a blended diet shake with fruit. While this regimen sounds fairly healthy, I made a game of trying to eat less and less.

This pattern was in place from Monday through Friday night when Bob and I would go out to eat to celebrate the weekend. I could hardly wait to eat whatever I wanted and to drink on that Friday night, because I knew I would purge afterward. On Saturday night, we had a few of the friends we had managed to make over or to go to their house. There, in the party atmosphere and less under anyone's watchful eye, I was able to eat and drink even more. Always hungover on Sunday, I would still make a nice dinner and perhaps have a glass of wine or two before starting the dance of deprivation all over again on Monday.

After a year of trying to secure a full-time teaching job, I decided to seek steady employment in another industry. I went to work as a client counselor for a company called HomeEquity. There were many displaced teachers and pilots working there. I made more friends and enjoyed the work and the comradery of being in an office.

There were many parties and dinners out as well as work functions where drinking was rampant. I thought I was drinking and eating like everyone else, but I'm sure my drunken binges did not go unnoticed. I remember one party at work where I stopped on the way home, got a dozen donuts, ate them all and threw them back up into the box before I got home. I put the box in a dumpster. While I tried to maintain my rigid routine, binging was not uncommon during the week. I continued to restrict my eating until I was all but starving myself throughout the week, and the less I ate, the more in control I felt. I had to have control to disguise how out of control I was on the weekends and even more significantly, on the inside.

What I know now is that I was incredibly lonely and depressed. By moving to Connecticut with Bob, I had been stripped of everything and everyone I used to identify myself. I had no positions, no close relationships, no status in my work or anywhere else. I made a few friends, but the amount Bob was gone left me alone a lot. I simply didn't know how to feel whole and content without those outside people and titles to tell me who I was. Instead of facing this fear, I continued to run from it. I escaped into alcohol and food, but instead of just binging and purging, I added starvation and became a full-blown Anorexic (yet another term unidentified at the time.)

This pattern of starving and binging eventually brought my weight to dangerously low levels. I thought about food all the time, and during my lunch breaks from work I would go to the library to look up recipes to prepare on the weekends. I weighed myself multiple times daily and was always elated when I had lost more. I had no idea how emaciated I looked, because all I saw was fat. If I gained weight, I panicked. Control of my weight seemed the only lifeline I had to feeling in control of my emotions, which were buried deep inside, under layers of fear, denial and self-will.

In the summer of 1977, Bob and I went back to Denver for my

ten-year high school reunion. I weighed 97 pounds on what should be about a 120-pound frame. When we showed up at the park for the picnic, a classmate I had been friends with since elementary school came up to me with what I can only describe as alarm on her face. "What has happened to you?" she asked. She was sure that I had cancer. I had no idea why she was asking me that until I thought about it afterward. She was horrified by my skeletal appearance.

Anorexia is a cunning foe. The victim has no idea they have it, and while I had a vague notion that what I was doing with food was not normal, I could find nothing in any publication that described my sick relationship with food. I mentioned to my doctor in Denver at one time that I purged occasionally. He looked at me and proclaimed that the Romans did that all the time. Case closed. I don't think Bob realized how emaciated I had become because the weight loss had been gradual, and he had gotten used to the way I looked. It was impossible, however, for me to hide my binge-purge pattern from Bob, and that, combined with my excessive sloppy drinking and eating at home and parties began to impact our marriage. Days following my weekend binges were not pleasant as Bob was embarrassed and unimpressed by my behavior.

My mom was concerned about how thin I was, but I viewed her as my hyper critical mom. My friend Wendy commented on my weight, but somehow her comments didn't register either. Yet when I saw the look of horror on my classmate's face, her reaction served as a mirror to what I really looked like. I came face to face with a woman who was withering away to nothing. I knew I needed to put a halt to losing more weight, though I still wasn't ready to gain weight.

The most puzzling thing about this period in my life is that I had absolutely no idea how lonely and depressed I had become. I continued to maintain an upbeat demeanor as I sank deeper and deeper into my addictions, compulsions and rigid structure. I fought to maintain control of my feelings and continued to pour more booze and food into the hole inside, hoping to fill it but only forcing it to grow larger and deeper.

7

Parallel Paths

As MUCH AS Bob and I loved our little cottage at the end of Saviano Lane, we were anxious to reinvest the equity from the sale of Bob's home in Denver. After several weeks of searching, we made an offer on a little house on an azalea-tree-lined block in nearby Fairfield, about 10 miles from our home in Westport. The more middle-class town suited us much better than affluent Westport, and we had hopes of making more friends there. After two years in our sweet Westport cottage, we made the move.

Across the street from our new house lived another young couple who were of similar age and ambition. Jim was an attorney and Cindy worked as well. Even though they were both from generations of New Englanders, they became good friends with whom we socialized on weekends. It was unusual for New Englanders to readily accept outsiders, so we were especially honored when they invited us to join them at a party at the Fairfield Hunt Club to which they belonged. I am quite sure they questioned the wisdom of their decision to include us after I took advantage of the open bar to the point of asking the band if they would like me to sing with them. In retrospect, I am quite sure they did NOT want me to sing with them, but thinking I might be a member, they conceded. Imagine Jim and Cindy's surprise when they found their guest serenading the gentrified of Fairfield with a slurred version of a song I still don't remember. Perhaps they were as drunk as I was, as I think they continued to see us after that.

My way of dealing with what should have been an embarrassing situation was just to make fun of myself and my drinking. I imagine I apologized to Jim and Cindy for my behavior, but I blamed my being "overserved" and basically laughed it off. I knew Bob wasn't too enthused about my debut to Cindy and Jim's friends, but I considered him overly concerned about what others thought and ignored his opinion. I wasn't ready to acknowledge how my drinking affected him and others and was committed to living my party life with abandoned. I wasn't big on people telling me what to do and considered my drinking a sign of my independence.

We really enjoyed Jim and Cindy, but our best friends in Connecticut were transplants like us. We met Wayne and Cindy through a gal I substitute taught with. Cindy's husband, Wayne, was an FBI agent. We immediately clicked with Wayne's quirky New Hampshire humor which was a perfect complement to Cindy's personable California openness. We all loved to eat and drink and shared many holidays and camping trips. It was not unusual to find Cindy and I passed out on the floor after a night of drinking. Cindy was my weight-control soul mate, so talking about weight concerns as much as we did made me feel more normal. The difference between us was that she did not take her weight concerns to the depths I did, nor did she suffer my level of dependence on alcohol. While Cindy watched what she ate, I was starving myself. Cindy loved to party, but I am quite certain that I drank two drinks to every one she had. I know Cindy did not obsess about food like I did.

In addition to going to the library to look at cookbooks during my lunch breaks, I loved to grocery shop. Most of my free time was spent thinking about what I was going to eat on the weekend or planning the next party that would allow me to drink and eat excessively and purge multiple times. When Bob travelled, I was more likely to binge during the week, but my primary binge/purge cycle was relegated to weekends. I was only able to manage the building anxiety that grew during the week as I continued to suppress my feelings of insignificance and loneliness by planning and fantasizing the weekend relief I would get through food and booze. I wouldn't have described it this way at the time, but I was a prisoner to my addictions. I had to eat at a certain time, had to know that a drink would be available when I was ready for it, had to stick to a more and more structured schedule and became less able to function well outside of my self-imposed routine. If my eating schedule was thrown off for any reason, I became increasingly anxious though I fought to hide that anxiety from others. I was sliding further and further into a pattern of self-destruction.

Bob and I and our friends all worked and played hard in those early years of marriage. One thing we all had in common besides our affinity for a good party was our desire to begin families. Eventually, California Cindy became pregnant. My main concern about her pregnancy was that I knew she would quit drinking which was problematic in that she was one of my best drinking buddies. Our neighbor Cindy, like me, was unable to conceive. Both of us ended up seeing fertility specialists. I found my way to a doctor at Yale School of Medicine who was considered a premier expert in the field of infertility.

Not surprisingly, my anorexia had prevented me from ovulating. It didn't take the doctor long to identify the effect my low weight was having on my ability to get pregnant, and while I don't remember him using the term *anorexic*, he told me bluntly I would have to gain weight if I was to conceive. My anorexia resisted this news, but I did manage to put on a few pounds, in addition to the 8 or 9 pounds I had gained after my high school reunion, over the coming months. Still, I was *forcing* myself to eat more as weight gain remained terrifying to me. I was still too thin to ovulate. I can only imagine the confusion my body was experiencing. I wanted to create another human being within a body I was actively attacking with alcohol and a lack of proper nutrition. I continued my regimen of weekly starvation followed by weekends of binge eating, purging, and drinking.

The doctor began prescribing fertility medications which had little effect. Weekly trips to New Haven to visit with the doctor continued, and after numerous medications failed, I began receiving injections of a fertility drug called Pergonal. I had just begun the injections when another big life change interrupted my treatments.

When I agreed to marry Bob, one of the conditions was a yearly review of our life in Connecticut. On our wedding anniversary each year, we made the decision to stay another year in Connecticut or move back to Colorado. After four years, we decided we had seen all we wanted to see of New England and were ready to return to the drier climate, majestic mountains and wide-open skies of Colorado. Luckily, Bob missed Colorado and the outdoors as much as I missed my friends and family. Bob began a job search, and it didn't take him long to land a position with a Johnson and Johnson subsidiary in Denver.

Ahhhh. I was thrilled and relieved to be returning to my roots and the security of the life I knew best. While I was still in denial about the toll the move to Connecticut had taken on me, I felt encouraged by our move home. I looked forward to a lovely new home, reconnection with our friends, and hopefully a family to begin this next chapter of our life.

Some of *my* plans were realized. But God's plans were bigger and pushed us into unchartered waters neither of us were prepared to navigate. Time to sink or learn to breathe under water.

8

Moving Parts

THERE ARE DEFINITE advantages to moving into a neighborhood of all new homes. Our Denver move found us purchasing a new home in a suburb south of Denver. Since everyone was new to the neighborhood, we were all quick to become friends. It was not difficult to identify the neighbors with whom we would become frequent partiers. There was at least one get together every weekend, and it wasn't unusual for some of us gals to get together for a "glass of wine" during the week. What *would* have been unusual for me would have been to actually have just one glass of wine.

Once we became settled in our new house, I was introduced to a nurse who would become a good friend. Dee came to our house to give me the injection of Pergonal I had begun taking in Connecticut as Bob and I continued to hope for children. We had decided to try at least one more injection but were beginning to consider adoption.

You might think returning home and being near my mom and old friends would have alleviated my need to manage my emotions through the rigid eating and drinking routine I had established . But by the time we returned, I was so entrenched in my addictive behaviors that the cycle of drinking-binging-purging on the weekends continued. Contributing to my depression was my fear of never conceiving a child, and while I knew my low weight was contributing to my infertility, I simply was incapable of breaking the cycle to which I had become addicted. I still obsessed about my weight and continued to be the party planner, ever organizing gatherings in order to experience the relief I needed with booze and food.

Addiction, as I eventually learned in recovery, is cunning, baffling and powerful. Because I was able to control my drinking and eating most of the time during the week, I convinced myself I really *was* in control. I believed I was choosing my behavior, when the truth was, I was completely under the control of alcohol and food. During the week, I was masking both what was eventually diagnosed as depression and the hole that grew inside until the weekend of relief arrived, as it did every single week. I didn't understand my depression as a physical condition, but continually berated myself for feeling down when I had so much to be grateful for. I believed it was my responsibility to work my way out of my feelings of listless sadness, and I attempted to escape those feelings by being busy and anticipating my next binge.

My life appeared typical in the world of young married couples. I worked in and outside of our home, I was making friends in the neighborhood and connecting with longtime friends from my childhood. But my mind was continually spinning. I was obsessed with alcohol and food. I spent hours poring over recipes, and I counted the days until the weekend when I could release my pent-up anxiety and relieve my depression by eating and drinking with abandon.

Not surprisingly, I became a gourmet cook. All that obsession with food and recipes culminated in me spending weekends preparing elaborate meals that included many of the foods I denied myself throughout the week. Bob loved to eat and was a fan of my emerging skills in the kitchen. I enjoyed the creative aspect of cooking and of course loved pairing the meals with good wines. Sometimes I would cook for just me and Bob or we would entertain as many as ten couples on the weekend. All of these gatherings were fun and provided me the perfect outlet for my binge, purge and drink fests.

The release I experienced on the weekends would be followed by regret on Monday, and I would once again commit myself to a regimented diet and one beer a night. The hangovers I usually had would steal whole days of my life from me as I spent the day recovering. There were a few times during a binge when I would actually throw up blood. I knew this pattern of living was unhealthy, but I had convinced myself that it was my normal and became the only way I knew how to live as my addictive demons continued to ravage my peace of mind and my self-esteem.

I got a job in the real estate industry, supporting agents who sold home warranties to home sellers. I worked from home and also travelled throughout the state. Bob found his job challenging and stimulating and we were both thrilled to live in such an active, friendly neighborhood. As I continued to ignore my self-destructive behavior, our lives seemed to be all that we had hoped for with the exception of our inability to conceive.

Bob grew up with parents he never saw argue in a house that seemed free of problems or conflict. Whatever issues his parents had were handled in private, and Bob's memories center around a fun, loving family. His family accepted me into the loving fold, and I learned almost everything I know about unconditional love and acceptance from them. Bob shared the unconditional love he had learned from his family with me and focused on the fun and mutual respect we had for each other.

We still argued about my drinking and binging and purging, but I believe Bob's lack of experience in dealing with conflict led him to mostly ignore the self-destructive path I was on. He just didn't know what to do with it, and the positive attitude he had naturally resulted in his focusing on the good things in our relationship, of which there were many. We talked about our desire to have kids and saw that as our biggest problem and focus.

On Valentine's Day of 1980, Bob and I went to dinner at a restaurant that had become a favorite. We were still romantic five years into our marriage, so we took advantage of this holiday to enjoy a night out together. After dinner, I handed Bob a box. Inside was a rattle – my way of announcing to him I was pregnant. He was overjoyed, as I knew he would be, and the next chapter of our life was beginning – delayed, but otherwise according to plan. As excited as I was to learn I was pregnant, the most precious moment was telling Bob. I remember the joy of sharing it with him as if it were yesterday. One of Bob's greatest assets is his absolute unbridled exuberance, and his reaction to the news brought tears to the eyes of our waitress. Finally, when I was 31 and he 32, the next chapter had begun.

9

Winken, Blinken and Nod

I WAS SICK. I was experiencing significant morning sickness that often lasted throughout the day, but I knew women experienced this unwelcome side effect, so nothing seemed unusual about this pregnancy. But at twelve weeks, I began spotting and went in for an ultrasound. I was worried about the baby, so when the ultrasound seemed to continue longer that it should have, I began to fear the worst.

The technician seemed to be taking her time which made me nervous, but she eventually told us what had been taking her so long. She discovered we were having twins. After that discovery she continued scanning as there seemed to be an indentation in the sac surrounding the babies. Further exploration revealed something we never dreamed of. The twins had a buddy. Triplets. That would be three...babies. Three little lives all at once. Three cribs, three bottoms to change, three mouths to feed. Three college educations. Three weddings. The fertility treatment had worked in a big way, and we now had an instant family to plan for. After considering we may never have children, the idea of three kids at once was a dream come true.

I think the reality of life with triplets hit me when we told my mom. I would describe her reaction as panic masquerading as joy. She had the kind of smile you see when someone tells their son-in-law they are coming to visit for a week. It is trying to say "oh, I can't wait" but really says "that long?" I was a bit confused as I was sure she would be as excited as we were, but I imagine she was thinking about how dramatically our lives were about to change, and also what it would mean for *her* as our main source of help and support since Bob's parents lived out of state. God love her.

True to form, I sprang into action. I hit every garage sale I could find looking for cribs, changing tables, diaper pails, etc. I managed to acquire the necessities and arrange the rooms for the litter to come. Our house was made for this tribe as we had three bedrooms across from our master bedroom upstairs, each with a dormer that faced the front of the house on our lovely cul-de-sac. It was meant to be.

My plan was to have two boys and one girl, and our name selections mirrored that plan. Boys' names seemed easy to come by, while we struggled more with names for girls, which seems a bit prophetic as I look back.

I was even willing to curtail my drinking. I read that one cup of wine would not hurt the babies, so I would measure a cup of wine, pour it in a jar, and take it with me when we went visit friends. I missed the release drinking gave me, but the knowledge that this was temporary sustained me. The thought of *not* drinking at all during my pregnancy was out of the question. I couldn't imagine my life without alcohol.

At 20 weeks, I could sense spasms that felt like what I imagined must be labor. A neighbor took me to the hospital where I was met by my doctor and given Terbutaline to arrest the labor. My OB-GYN, Dr. Engel, decided bedrest would be mandatory if these kids were to remain in utero long enough to survive, so my new place of residence became our bedroom in which Bob placed a small refrigerator, television and phone. With the internet not yet on the scene, I remember watching all of Wimbledon that summer, reading lots of books, writing letters and enjoying visitors. The days were long, and the bigger I got, the more difficult it was to sleep. My focus on the babies distracted me from the feelings of emptiness I normally experienced without my weekend release routine.

Feeling the babies move inside of me was an experience I will always treasure. I would lay my hands on my swelling body and imagine which baby was moving, what each baby looked like, and how they were developing. I dreamed about the kids they would become, the friendship they would have with each other, and the joy we would experience watching them navigate this life as they revealed their little personalities to us. I planned how we would raise them and gave myself way too much credit for how they would turn out based on our excellent parenting.

I was counting down the days until October, but on July 30, I again went to the hospital with premature labor pains. The Terbutaline was not effective this time as these babies were determined to make their entrance twelve weeks early. That should be okay, right? I heard about a woman who had her triplets at 27 weeks, and they were all doing fine.

I was transported by ambulance from Rose Medical Center to University Hospital for the delivery. Rose did not have a Neonatal Intensive Care Unit (NICU) for newborns in 1980, and these babies would need that level of care. When I was rolled into the delivery room, I was greeted by over 30 doctors, nurses and residents who were excited to witness a multiple birth. I was awake during the C-section when we met our three beautiful, pink, noisy babies. First out came tiny, 2-lb, 6-oz Jared. Next was 2-lb, 8-oz Adam. And finally, we met 2-lb, 12-oz Greg. Our first indication that things may not go as I had planned – three boys.

I was in awe at the sight of these little humans emerging from me. Comprehending the mystery of the life emerging from what was a very crowded incubator defined the word miracle for me in dramatic fashion. I could not wait to hold my boys, to feed and create for them the kind of family I had always wished for. I was confident Bob and I would be great parents to these three healthy, thriving boys. The delivery was complete; let the parenting begin.

After rearranging my insides and sewing them back into my body (which Bob watched in its entirety – who does that?), Bob and I were escorted into the ICU to get acquainted with our sweet boys. I could hardly wait to witness the perfect, angelic faces of the new lives that had just emerged from my womb.

What we saw instead were three tiny, precious boys who were not ready to leave the protected sanctity of their cocoon. They weren't "done." Bob and I were also unprepared for the sight of these fragile, not-yet-finished babies, each intubated with wires and monitors covering their little bodies. I had trouble comprehending the meaning of this picture. We knew there were risks with premature delivery, but we chose to believe the best and did not prepare ourselves for the harsh reality that ensued.

You would think there may have been some sadness and grieving going on at this point, but all I remember is being on high alert for the decisions that needed to be made and the news that we would receive each day. I was numb. I was recovering from surgery and trying to connect to these babies all at the same time. It was overwhelming.

The following days and weeks were a blur of decisions and diagnoses. Our emotions were up and down. I remember one night going to our room and beating on a pillow while I cried, terrified about the future and frustrated by the lack of knowing. Lack of knowing what interventions were most helpful for our boys, lack of knowing the outcome, and lack of knowing if we could handle this.

We learned quickly that the two most common concerns for premature infants were cerebral hemorrhage due to underdeveloped ventricles in the brain, and hyaline membrane disease from underdeveloped lungs. Each day, the doctors would suggest possible symptoms of both these conditions for all the boys, but after a few days it became clear Greg was struggling with his lungs and Adam had likely had a significant cerebral hemorrhage. We spent our days at the hospital and only went home to sleep at night. Fluid began accumulating in Adam's head, further indicating the presence of a bleed. Tubes were inserted into Greg's chest, and he remained intubated to help him breathe on his own. Jared only seemed to need support with his low levels of oxygen.

We consulted frequently with doctors and nurses, seeking answers to questions that remained unanswerable. Would our boys be okay? What were the possible prognoses based on what they were experiencing? What can you do to help them? Each day brought new challenges, but it became clear that Adam must have relief from the fluid accumulating in his brain if he was to survive. The initial plan was to embark on a series of spinal taps, an incredibly painful procedure that would be performed every day for five days. Greg, in the meantime, continued to fight to breath with little success.

In an effort to protect myself emotionally during these tumultuous early days, I found myself alternately surrendering and pulling back my full engagement with each of the boys. When one would seem critical, I found myself attaching to the other two. Since each day introduced a different scenario, I was reluctant to fully commit to any of them. I loved them all, but I had learned at a very early age not to get too close to anyone. Hurt was painful and lasting, and I reverted to my protective instincts as I steeled myself for the daily reports. It felt strange and wrong to be emotionally responding so randomly, but after learning as a child that those trips to Disneyland were never going to happen, that my dad was never going to quit drinking and that my mom was too fragile to lean on, all I knew to do was to protect myself from the pain. Of course, when the emotions became overwhelming, I could always drink and eat them away which I did on the weekends as I fell back into my established pattern.

The doctors began what was to become a futile series of spinal taps to relieve the fluid in Adam's brain. Watching him endure this procedure was agonizing but it paled in comparison to what came next.

In the middle of the night on August 9, on our fifth wedding anniversary, we were called to the hospital to make a life-or-death decision for Greg. We were speeding to the hospital when we were pulled over by a police officer who sympathetically escorted us the rest of the way. We were gazing through tears at the road ahead as we contemplated the decision before us. I don't think we said a word.

I remember entering a room where a team was gathered to tell us Greg was deteriorating. We had to decide whether to employ heroic measures to keep him breathing or to let him go. We were told further intervention would not guarantee he would live, and even if he did, his life would be highly compromised. We both knew we didn't want to relegate Greg to a life of pain and struggle. It was time to let him go. I held his tiny body, wrapped in a yellow blanket, for the last time that night. I remember looking down at his perfect face and realizing how precious and miraculous and fragile life is. Greg lost his battle that night, and we lost a piece of our family and our heart.

In my search for serenity and a spiritual foundation for our kids, Bob and I began regularly attending church. While our faith was not a big part of our lives at that time, Bob and I both had enough faith to believe Greg was now in heaven and we would see him again.

When I got pregnant, we began attending St. Andrews United Methodist Church which had an accepting message and a kind pastor. Fortunately, at St. Andrews, there was plenty of room for questioning and interpretation of the Bible. Bob and I had both been raised in the church and wanted our family to be involved in a faith-based community.

I remember feeling guilty on Sundays as I nursed yet another hangover while enthusiastically singing the hymn of the day. I believed there was a God but felt removed and certainly not reliant on Him. I was negotiating terms with Him. Though I was raised a Christian, I questioned many of the tenants of the faith and my prayers were to a God I couldn't fully identify. I admired those who had great faith, but I truly did not think I could ever embrace that kind of trust after my experiences with trust in my childhood. I thought God was essentially unavailable to me and me to Him.

Our pastor came to visit us a few different times after the kids were born, and he was a great comfort when Greg died. He assured us of Greg's place in heaven, but I still recall seeing a look of perplexed pain in his eyes. Not that we were looking for the answer to why this had happened to Greg, but I could tell he wanted to find the words to make sense of our sorrow. He couldn't find the words, but he prayed and grieved with us which was a tender demonstration of the love of God.

10

The Road Home

MEANWHILE, THE AMOUNT of fluid accumulating in the ventricles of Adam's brain became alarming. It was suggested that Adam needed a shunt, which is a valve inserted into the ventricle that redirects the fluid through a tube that empties into the peritoneal cavity near the abdomen. This procedure would be performed at Children's Hospital and would be Adam's only chance for survival. It needed to happen soon.

Both Adam and Jared were transported by ambulance to Children's Hospital and the shunt was surgically inserted into Adam's little brain by the inventor of the device, Dr. Robert Hendee. The shunt had been an option for only ten years, and we feel blessed to this day Dr. Hendee had the foresight to create a mechanism that would allow children formerly referred to as Mongoloid to live and thrive.

Adam responded well to the surgery and was in recovery before we had the opportunity to pause and say goodbye to Greg. As lovers of the Colorado outdoors, we wanted Greg to rest in a natural setting, so we purchased plots for four of us (assuming Jared would have his own family and be buried elsewhere and Adam would likely not have a family of his own) in Evergreen Cemetery, a bucolic, natural cemetery in the hills of Evergreen. Our family, close friends and pastor gathered to lay Greg to rest in his little coffin, next to the grave of a dear friend's dad who had died the year before. It was good to have this brief time to focus on Greg as the whirlwind surrounding our other boys continued to swirl. We certainly did not have time to thoroughly grieve Greg but knowing he was safely contained in a place that was ours to visit and join him in some day was comforting.

While our hearts lingered at Greg's graveside, our minds were quickly pulled back to the immediate needs of Jared and Adam. Once it was determined Adam was healing well, both boys were transferred to yet another hospital to continue the observation and care that would allow them to come home. What seemed like a month had been just a few weeks when the boys met the staff at St. Luke's who were kind and encouraging, and the days turned into weeks as we settled into our routine. After Bob left for work each morning, I would head to the hospital to get the report from the night before. I can still remember the smell of the nursery as I walked in to greet our sweet, tiny boys. The smell was slightly medicinal, but it was mostly blankets and lotions and milk that created the baby aroma that pulled me into the world of my children. The room was warm, and I often found the boys sporting hand knitted caps or covered in homemade blankets when I arrived. After what seemed like continual triage right after they were born, this environment was far less stressful.

Later in the afternoon, I would return home, make dinner for Bob and me, then we would both go back to the hospital for our evening visit. Between visits, I spent many hours pumping my breasts to provide enough milk to last both boys between visits. Adam was unable to create the suction necessary to nurse, but once Jared began to nurse successfully, we started anticipating the day our boys would come home. After two months in the hospital, Jared was discharged.

I love to say that Jared disclosed his personality from the day he was born. The only reason he was in the hospital for two months is because he was unable or unwilling to wean himself from the quarter liter of oxygen he needed to maintain the required levels. The amount of oxygen he needed was the difference between Denver and sea level. He was comfortable and in no hurry to move on. He has continued to display that very unhurried, laid-back personality ever since. He began talking later than most kids, but in almost complete sentences from the minute he opened his mouth. He was not a great student until college when he could pursue the things that interested him after which he excelled. We bought him a car for Christmas when he was sixteen, and he didn't drive it for six months. I love that Jared immediately showed us the inherent "Jaredness" that would shape his life, regardless of how much we tried to hurry him. I believe it was the first of many life lessons we learned in raising our boys.

After Jared's emotional homecoming at the end of September, we began the tricky process of dividing our time between the hospital and home. I bundled little Jared in warm outfits to prepare him for the crisp autumn days that accompanied us to and from the hospital. Adam continued to grow stronger, and the joy and humor that would define him for years to come was revealed a little more each day. The critical days were behind us, and the days that followed were more about patience than fear. Adam had to remain in the hospital and he continued to recover from the shunt surgery and build the strength he needed to thrive at home. Three months after he was born, Adam was finally discharged on Halloween.

I brought a pumpkin-decorated cake to the nursery to thank the kind nurses who had adored and cared for Adam and Jared for the past few months. We watched Adam go through his final evaluations, and eventually sat down with a doctor from his pediatric group after dressing him in his homecoming outfit. We were sitting in a small, cramped office just outside the unit when the doctor matter-of-factly told us: "Adam has cerebral palsy. It is hard to assess the severity at this time, but he may never walk, never talk or feed himself. Then again, at the other end of the spectrum, you may barely be able to tell that he has CP." What? I reminded myself to breathe. What was the doctor saying? How were we supposed to process this information? The pure joy we felt when taking Jared home was very different with Adam. Adam's homecoming was joy-filled, but with that joy also came fear, uncertainty and many, many questions. We knew it was possible

Adam would have some special needs, but the diagnosis of cerebral palsy was one that held a depth and weight we were unprepared for. We hadn't imagined our lives with wheelchairs or feeding tubes or any of the other challenges we had seen associated with a child with complicated mobility issues like cerebral palsy.

Bringing Adam home to complete our family was both a welcome and tender milestone. Determining our daily routine was a constant work in progress, but we loved our boys and found something new to celebrate about them each day. We shared the nightly feedings, and I soon learned that Bob was all over the 5 a.m. feeding because there were re-runs of the Lone Ranger on at that time. Sleep, as is true with any baby, was at a premium.

Our visits to the pediatrician included good news about the boy's health but were also peppered with our anxious questions about how we could best help Adam. We wanted to be as pro-active as we could with Adam, but we were clueless. Fortunately, Jerry Rubin, Adam and Jared's primary pediatrician, was compassionate and informed, and he suggested we begin physical, occupational and speech therapy with Adam as soon as he was six months old to help him maximize his potential.

Since we didn't know the severity of Adam's disabilities, we dove in to find answers and to help him thrive. Cerebral palsy is a group of disorders that affect movement and muscle tone or posture. It's caused by damage that occurs to the immature brain as it develops, most often before birth, but in Adam's case, immediately after birth.

In general, cerebral palsy causes impaired movement associated with abnormal reflexes, floppiness or rigidity of the limbs and trunk, abnormal posture, involuntary movements, unsteady walking, or some combination. People with cerebral palsy can have problems swallowing and commonly have eye muscle imbalance, in which the eyes don't focus on the same object. They also might have reduced range of motion at various joints of their bodies due to muscle stiffness. Cerebral palsy's effect on function varies greatly. Some affected people can walk; others need assistance. Some people show normal or near-normal intellect, but others have intellectual disabilities. Epilepsy, blindness or deafness also might be present.

Physical, Occupational and Speech therapy were designed to treat all the different symptoms of CP. The therapy world was a whole new adventure for us. We began Adam's therapy journey at Children's Hospital where we saw a physical therapist (PT) once a week. Soon, we had connected with an occupational therapist (OT) who came to our home once a week. When he was a bit older, he began seeing a speech therapist (ST) as well. When I took Adam to therapy, I would drop Jared at my mom's house. A year or so after we began these therapies, Adam began attending an early intervention program for children with special needs that also provided therapy in addition to the therapies he was receiving through individual therapists. Adam attended a preschool for children with special needs while Jared was in a co-op preschool. Our lives seemed to center around Adam's therapies in those days, and each therapist wanted us to spend time outside of therapy working with him as well.

It is safe to say that Bob and I were overwhelmed. We never felt we were doing enough for Adam, and we also desperately wanted him to have time to just be a *kid*. We continued to adapt our family activities to include Adam and live our lives as normally as we could.

One of the first conclusions we came to when putting together the Adam puzzle was that speech was *not* going to be a problem for him. He talked early and often, and his vocabulary far exceeded his understanding of his words. Discipline became difficult to enforce when Adam, in a moment of indignation, called me a "grassy meadow." Another time he claimed that I was a "typewriter" for not giving in to one of his demands. He was usually so mellow and happy, but his frustrations at not being able to move well resulted in the wrath of his vocabulary. It was pretty hilarious most of the time. We learned that kids compromised in one part of their brain or body often compensate in another area. For Adam, it was speech. That kid could talk.

I continued to assume the role of strong, capable woman and took my life with infant twins, one needing a lot of additional care, in stride.

I was always tired and remember one late afternoon when I had both boys sitting on the counter in their infant seats crying, trying to get them to drink from their bottles. I was exhausted from not only caring for them, but from fighting to continue conforming to my ridged rules for eating and drinking. On this day, I made up for what the boys wouldn't eat by drinking a few beers and eating a box of Triscuits, crying right along with them. If you can't beat 'em, join 'em.

11

The Village

I DIDN'T ALWAYS enjoy the hassle of taking Adam to therapy appointments or cleaning up after his projectile vomiting. I wasn't a fan of changing his diapers until he was six years old and carrying him around as much as I did was tiring. But these and the countless extra tasks involved with all things Adam were overshadowed by his ready laugh, his hilarious comments and the joy that always emanated from that mischievous face and those big blue eyes.

We made the necessary adaptations for Adam when we did things as a family. Hiking meant putting Adam in a pack on Bob's back while our family blazed the trails of the Colorado mountains we so loved. The stroller was always on standby for amusement parks, walks and visits to friends and family. Visits to the park or swimming pool required extra hands-on help for Adam. The double stroller was awkward, but it was a life saver on long walks and visits to the mall where I was able to relieve the stress of busy days with a little retail therapy and a coffee ice cream cone which I managed to work into my rigid eating plan during the week. The question was never *if* we would engage in activities; the question was *how* we would make the experience work for Adam.

As I look back on our daily routine in those early years, I am grateful that both Jared and Adam loved books. Every afternoon, before naptime, I would sit on the couch flanked by two eager bookworms and read. It wasn't long before the boys could recite the pages of their favorite books, and we spent many joyful hours poring over books like *On Market Street* with its intricate illustrations, the scary adventures of Max in *Where the Wild Things Are*, or the strange but captivating images in *Goodnight Moon*.

Creating a typical family environment for our kids was challenging with all the therapies and medical appointments Adam required. What began as weekly visits to therapists grew into participation in a network of agencies and individuals providing services for children with special needs. Follow-up doctor appointments related to Adam's shunt and considerable orthopedic procedures related to his cerebral palsy in addition to normal pediatrician appointments became the norm.

The early intervention program in which Adam participated for three years provided occupational, speech and physical therapies overseen by an early intervention specialist, Miss Jo. Since Jared had been diagnosed with speech delays (which I now believe were more a choice than a delay) he was able to participate with Adam for a time in early intervention. I remember taking the boys to "school," then packing a picnic and going to the nearby park afterward on warm fall and spring days.

Over the first year of Adam's life, a village grew around us. There was Diane, his physical therapist, Cindy, his occupational therapist, and for a brief time, a speech therapist whose name escapes me. His medical team included his pediatrician Dr. Rubin, orthopedic surgeon Dr. Chang, and neurosurgeon Dr. Hendee in addition to the orthopedist who would create plastic braces for Adam's legs and other specialists with whom we consulted. We connected with Developmental Pathways, the organization that would manage the services he was entitled to through the Medicaid waiver, which provides supports to individuals with special needs.

This village was integral to the roadmap that would lead Adam to become his best. While we relied on the numerous medical and early development professionals to guide us on Adam's developmental journey, it was our friends and family we leaned on for emotional support. These were the same people with whom we shared support raising Jared.

Bob and I never felt like we were doing enough for Adam. We left every therapy session with a suggested plan of action for daily work with Adam. Ideally, we would have been working with Adam for three hours a day on feeding, mobility and fine motor skills. Our therapists were wonderful, but did not communicate with each other, so all the treatment Adam was getting was segregated from the other therapies he received. We continually struggled with the question of how much to therapize Adam vs. how much time he should be allowed to just be a kid. We were overwhelmed, underprepared, and perpetually feeling guilty. We were exhausted.

I can't imagine navigating this journey without the direction and encouragement of those who have been working, caregiving and directing others down this path with no clear destination. Would Adam walk? Would he be able to learn, go to college, work? Would he live with us for the rest of his life? There was no roadmap for Adam. Our goals were to make him as "normal" as possible. We had so much to learn about "normal" and even more to learn about who was ultimately in charge of the outcomes of Adam's and our lives.

While Adam required so much from us, we tried to stay diligent in meeting Jared's needs and wants. I worked alongside other parents at his co-op preschool. We were lucky to have many families in our neighborhood with young children, and in fact identified six other sets of twins. Jared played with many of the neighborhood kids, and I became close friends with several of their moms. Our neighborhood of young moms worked out our parenting inexperience and insecurities by trading stories and commiserating with each other about the challenges of different developmental stages. Those conversations were comforting, encouraging and helpful.

Everyone who has raised kids knows this job is not for sissies. But raising Adam took that expression to another level altogether. There was comfort in the sameness of parenting when it came to Jared. If my neighbor's kid had started to walk and Jared was about the same age and starting to walk, I felt good about that. If Jared was riding a bike and my neighbor's child learned to ride a bike too, that gave us yet another experience to share. When Jared became friends with other kids his age, we felt we were raising a socially appropriate child. Certainly there can be competition among parents, but for the most part, I think our neighborhood of families encouraged and reassured each other.

Very little about Adam's development was the same as the neighborhood kids. He didn't walk when they did. He didn't eat like they did. He certainly couldn't learn his letters or colors like they did. He couldn't run or ride bikes with the other kids, so while he was well loved, developing friendships with them was not his reality. As we continued to navigate Adam's "specialness," we felt isolated in managing the unique challenges he presented.

A big contributing factor to these differences was his immobility. Adam never crawled. He scooted on his elbows, which led to his nickname Scooter which stuck for a few years. Much of the time he spent with his physical therapist, Diane was devoted to strengthening his weak core, which was the main culprit in his instability. His behaviors were different: he was still scooting after and biting his brother when he was five and six years old. He had poor impulse control and would melt down more easily and often than Jared. His frustration with his lack of mobility resulted in him acting out more as well. His weak gag reflex and sensitivity to certain foods meant continued projectile vomiting well into his toddler years. He was not potty trained at five years old. Our friends were kind and supportive, but parenting Adam began to feel lonely. Even though we accepted Adam's disability, we felt more and more inadequate as we watched the developmental gaps between Jared and Adam grow.

Making adaptations for Adam became our daily challenge, but we were encouraged by his slow but steady progress. He was gradually developing the skills that would allow him to be more independent, and any notion that he would be unable to care for himself began to fade. We were really beginning to dream of the possibilities for Adam.

Then, it was time to go to school. Early intervention was one thing. Pre-kindergarten was something quite different.

When we went to visit the school he was to attend, it was obvious that his scooting around the linoleum floor in the public-school classroom would not work. The teachers and staff suggested the dreaded word: wheelchair. Never had we considered Adam using a wheelchair for mobility. Walking, if he was able to, would be hard for Adam initially. Why would he walk if someone would push him around? We were at a crossroads.

By this time, Adam had been diagnosed as Hemiplegic, which is actually one-sided cerebral palsy. His right side was impacted. Because of his able left side, there was great promise he would walk. We needed to find a way to help him meet that milestone soon.

Diane suggested we try an innovative therapy she had learned about. She knew of a woman who offered intensive physical therapy in her home in Aspen. Parent and child would stay with her for a week while she provided five hours a day of intensive therapy to the child for five consecutive days. We decided that the therapy was worth taking a chance on, so Jared, Adam and I packed up and went to live with Maureen, the physical therapist, for a week in her home. She worked Adam hard and he was exhausted at the end of each day, but he was making progress. She manipulated his legs, force him to bear weight, twisted and moved his body in ways that would prepare and strengthen his trunk and utilized other techniques she had learned to actually prepare him to utilize all he needed to walk.

At the end of the week, we met with Maureen and Adam to talk about the progress they had made. To my complete amazement, Adam took several steps in a walker. Seeing him upright and moving after only five days of therapy seemed miraculous. I had to admit I had been a bit skeptical about the amount of change that could occur in such a short time. But standing before me in his little walker was the evidence. What an encouraging blessing.

12

What About Us?

MY PERSONAL LIFE during these years was a precarious balancing act. In addition to the challenges life with a child with special needs presented, my mother was diagnosed with breast cancer shortly after the kids were born. She had felt a lump in her breast before the birth of the triplets, but put off addressing it for fear of adding to the stress in my life. I know she delayed for my sake, but because she waited, the tumor was larger and the cancer more advanced than we had hoped

We soldiered through the difficult times as we always had: with determination, humor and denial. The humor actually served all of us well, because sometimes you just had to laugh. I was determined to never become a victim, so I took what seemed like the best action during difficult times and tried to see the humor in the situation. One of the things that attracted me most to Bob in the first place was his great sense of humor, and there were many times when we leaned on laughter through some difficult experiences. But sometimes, life just wasn't funny.

When I took Adam to the hospital in the middle of the night to have neurosurgery when his shunt failed and Bob was out of town, that wasn't funny. When my mother was diagnosed with bone cancer four years into remission, we didn't laugh. Adam's continued hospitalizations with shunt issues and orthopedic surgeries were not humorous.

During those times especially, my primary coping strategy of eating and drinking my stress away accelerated. In order to set up situations where I could drink and eat with abandon, I continued my role as party planner. Our neighborhood group were great partiers, some of whom currently exhibit or have since died from the disease of alcoholism. A small group of the most hard-core women among us would often gather in the afternoon for happy hour which often lasted well into the night after our husbands returned from work. Friday and Saturday nights were for drinking, eating and partying. I would like to say all the partying took place in our neighborhood, but that was not the case. I remember standing in the pouring rain, drunk and stoned, at Red Rocks belting out *What a Fool Believes* with the Doobie Brothers. We often drove to the mountains with picnics, beer and wine only to drive home drunk. Drive downtown to Octoberfest, drive home drunk. It wasn't like we had a designated driver. We all drank and drove. In retrospect, we were protected, as were those around us. Our kids were home with babysitters who were the older kids of some of the neighbors we partied with.

We had some great times during those years, but I know now I did not plan these gatherings solely for the fellowship. I desperately needed a release from the fear, exhaustion and anxiety that had been building inside me throughout the week. If I had been fighting demons before having kids, the added responsibility and lack of sleep that came with parenting and caring for my mom ramped up my desperate need to control and my constant feelings of being out of control. My worry for Adam and constant feelings of inadequacy in meeting his needs compounded my feelings of being out of control. Not being available for my mom as much as I would like to have been caused me guilt and still more anxiety.

My strength in the midst of the storm was accompanied by the suppression of all I was feeling. I stored my emotions throughout the week only to drink, binge and purge them away on the weekends. Often, I would binge and purge a few times during the week as well. Whether I was tired, angry, fearful or frustrated, my solution was to anesthetize those emotions with food and/or booze. I was determined to remain in perfect control of my family, but most of all of my emotions and my feelings. I was oblivious to the fact that I was relinquishing all my control to my addictions. I spent hours trying to manage my cravings for food and booze while also spending those hours planning for the next binge. I was locked in a pattern of destruction. I denied the impact my behavior was having on my body as it continued to recover from drunken binges only to repeat the process a few times the following weekend. I laughed at the antics like singing into the fireplace poked in someone's family room or driving up on the sidewalk at the grocery store to buy ice cream. I minimized the arguments with Bob that accompanied my drunken weekends. Most of all, I had no idea I had created a self-inflicted prison.

Meanwhile, Bob was focused on his career. His mid-west roots ingrained in him a strong sense of responsibility as the bread winner, and he was diligent. He was always willing to be with the kids on weekends so I could get out of the house for a few hours and was very hands on as a dad. We had the usual conflicts about who would do what when he was home, but I was clearly in charge of the kids and our household, a role I gladly accepted since I had chosen not to work once our kids were born. Bob enjoyed the fun we had with our friends, but the partying was never the elixir for him it had become for me. There were many times Bob would be less than thrilled after once again observing my pattern of overeating and throwing up in the neighbor's toilet, sometimes multiple times. It wasn't unusual for me to become a sloppy, slurring drunk. In my mind, I was having the fun I deserved after a hard week with kids and deprivation.

Bob's job came with generous benefits including membership in an upscale health club. I was able to take the kids to the club's childcare while I worked out. This was probably the first time I introduced a healthy coping self-care strategy into my life. Exercise definitely helped me curtail my eating and drinking cravings, though it was only one piece of the puzzle that would become the solution to this insanity.

We continued to attend church at St. Andrews, and I continued to be drawn to the idea that there was something greater than me that may have the power to bring comfort to my chaos. I prayed. While I was disconnected from whatever entity was hearing those prayers, I had not completely rejected God. By this time, my lifestyle was troubling and frustrating to me. My efforts to control how much I ate and drank failed me time after time. I became increasingly desperate to control my episodes of binge eating, and it became clear I was unable to do this on my own.

Once I realized I was unable to change the behaviors that had become my prison, that prison began to unravel. I was gaining a small glimpse of my powerlessness. I had disguised that prison so well behind a beautiful home, a husband and kids who loved me, and the latest hairstyle. While I wore my alcoholism as a badge of honor, bragging about how much I could drink, I tried to hide my eating disorders. I carried shame about both my drinking and bulimia, but since drinking was socially acceptable, I flippantly called myself an alcoholic to imply I was *choosing* to drink the way I did. My behavior reflected something different as my greatest resolve to modify it proved no match for my addictions. I needed help.

When the boys were around five years old, I took stock of the effect my behavior might have on my kids because of how it impacted me as their mother. I decided to see a therapist about my eating disorder. It wasn't long before she challenged me to look at my drinking as a factor that weakened my resolve and facilitated excessive binging and purging which was undeniable. Looking back, I can see that while I knew I drank too much, I simply could not imagine my life without alcohol, so I chose to deny it was a significant problem. Since I believed I *chose* to drink the way I did I had no interest in changing. Yet viewing my drinking in light of my eating disorder, I could see there was no way I could address one affliction without dealing with the other. I did not want my kids to grow up with a bulimic, alcoholic mother...which is exactly what I had become.

I found a therapist who had some experience with eating disorders who gently recommended AA and I made the decision to attend a meeting. I wanted to learn to drink responsibly so I could manage my binging episodes more effectively. What I heard loud and clear in that meeting was that a real alcoholic cannot drink responsibly. My interpretation of that was, "Alcoholics like YOU (the other people in the room) all cannot drink responsibly. I'm sure your alcoholism is much worse than mine, and besides, I'm not sure any of you are telling the truth about your sobriety." I looked at the steps posted on the wall and decided to stay and listen.

I attended a number of meetings over the next year or so and began to pay attention to the message of hope. I saw the peace and serenity that had so eluded me my entire life on the faces of many of the old-timers. I watched other people get sober. I could stay sober for a few weeks but was not yet convinced this way of life was for me. In the first place, it was suggested you get a sponsor to guide you through the steps, and I was quite sure I could select and work the steps I thought applied to me on my own. I still believed this program was a way to help me get control of my life, even though the first step talked about "powerlessness." I may have needed help, but I was a long way from admitting I was powerless.

I continued therapy and attending meetings and gained more awareness, including the notion that I was sick rather than bad or weak. While that relieved me of some of the guilt I was feeling, I was still not ready to acknowledge the power my addictions had in my life. I still believed the answer to my problems was greater self-knowledge that would enable me to control my behavior.

I didn't know it at the time, but I had begun a journey that would change my life in ways I could never have imagined. I would cross paths with incredible people who, by example, would reveal a way of life to me that was far better than any I had known. Most importantly, the elusive God who remained at arm's length to me for so long would gently wind His way into those hardened crevices of my wounded heart and began to reveal His healing power and love.

13

Mysterious Ways

THE YEAR 1986, when the kids were 6 years old, began with little fanfare. But three significant events would take place that year that would change not only our current circumstances, but the trajectory of our lives forever.

The first was my mother's passing from the cancer that had invaded her breast and then her bones over the past six years. Her death was a relief to her and also to me as it had become so difficult to watch her suffer. My brother came from California for her funeral and to help us move her few belongings from the assisted living facility she had called home for about a year. We laid her to rest in the family plot at Crown Hill Cemetery in Denver where she joined my dad, her brother and sister and her parents. My father had been gone for 21 years, and while their relationship had been battered and bruised by my dad's alcoholism, seeing them reunited was comforting. My mom had been lonely since his death.

Since I felt responsible for everyone in my life, my mom's loneliness felt like my problem to solve. I never thought I spent enough time with her. She had friends and family she saw occasionally, but I had come to believe she lived her life through me. My mom lost her mom when she was 12, and I am sure that impacted the development of her own self-concept. She was insecure and relied on comparing herself to others to gain self-worth. I know she loved me dearly, but she lived as a victim of her circumstance.

My relationship with my mom was complicated. Although I called her every day and saw her every weekend, I often heard her disappointment in our conversations. I couldn't do, couldn't say, couldn't be the person she needed. If you have known someone with a martyr mentality, you have heard the conversation.

"Hi mom! How are you?"

"Oh, I'm ok." It's important to get the tone of voice here. It's flat and definitely implies that she is NOT ok.

"So what are you doing today?"

"Oh, nothing." Same tone of voice. "What are you doing?"

"Well, I am working at the Jared's preschool, doing therapy with Adam, laundry, dinner, grocery shopping, etc."

Pause. This is the part where I am feeling guilty for something, but I'm not exactly sure what.

When Mom sacrificed her health to defer to my well-being, my guilt intensified. Surgery and chemotherapy were a part of her treatment, and I took her to appointments and helped as much as I could. Eventually, her disease went into remission for a time but required vigorous monitoring. This was a tough time for my mom, and it was emotionally exhausting for me as I tried to stay positive and helpful while dealing with my own feelings of guilt and inadequacy.

The day she died, I was volunteering at Jared's pre-school. She was in hospice, and I had called that morning to check on her. The nurses assured me they would call when she was nearing the end, but the end arrived sooner than expected. In 1986, there were no cell phones. The hospice was able to reach Bob at work, and when I saw him walk through the door of the pre-school, I knew. My mom had died, and I hadn't been there to hold her hand. I felt, in her final moments, I had let her down again and was sad I wasn't with her when she took her final breath.

The second event of 1986 that impacted us was the sale of the company Bob worked for. He had to find a new job. His best opportunity was with a company in Dallas, Texas, and we made the decision to move that summer. Neither of us was crazy about moving, but now that my mom was gone, we had the freedom to make that choice. The economy in Denver was not good during the oil and gas downturn, so we moved to support our family and Bob's career.

Before we left Denver, a friend Bob had worked with invited us to dinner to meet his neighbors who had lived in Dallas and had a daughter who still resided there. We were hoping to learn more about the city, where the best schools were located and other tips about living in that vibrant metropolis. That neighbor was Haddon Robinson.

Haddon Robinson was a great man of the Christian faith. He was President of Denver Seminary at the time and had served on the faculty of Dallas Seminary for many years before that. He authored several books, and eventually went on to host an Evangelical radio program. We didn't know anything about Haddon and his lovely wife Bonnie at the time. We viewed them as a generous pastor and his wife who had welcomed these strangers into their home to tell us about Dallas. This dinner led to a far greater connection than the connection to a Texas city.

The Robinsons encouraged me to call their daughter Vicki Hitzges, which I did shortly after our dinner together. When I called her, I could immediately tell that she was vivacious, strong and fun – my kind of woman. We talked about getting together when we arrived in Dallas, and the connection with her made me feel a bit better about once again leaving the town I had grown up in, though separating from our friends and great neighborhood was difficult.

After we arrived in Dallas and unpacked, I called Vicki. We quickly set a time to get together – she was welcoming and big as life. Vicki worked on TV and as a speaker and had a full life, but she was so willing to make time to introduce us to the city she loved. Vicki was authentic and funny and real....and she was a Christian who loved Jesus. Among the tips she gave me was the name of the church she attended which was Northwest Bible Church. In continuation of our spiritual journey, our family began attending services there. I joined a women's Bible Study Vicki was a part of, and I began to re-examine the faith I had questioned. I watched Vicki and others seek to live lives devoted to God, and I began to feel the pull of Christ on my heart. It was more of a whisper than a tug, but the notion that there was peace and forgiveness available to me through a spiritual connection began to seem possible. I believe accepting I needed help in my life may have opened me up again to that notion. The Christ being revealed to me was a different man than the one presented on the green felt boards in the Sunday School classes of my youth. This re-defined Christ was more than a supreme score keeper who multiplied fish and turned over the tables in the temple to expose and condemn sin.

I began to view God as a friend; a perfect power whose attributes of love and grace were not motivated by His desire to punish and control me but were fueled by His intense desire to be in relationship with His child. I began to pray with the knowledge that God's love for me was meant not to manipulate me into someone I'm not, but to guide and empower me to become the woman He had created me to be. I began to understand I was created with purpose, and my gifts and talents were not great accomplishments on my part, but were gifts given to me by this loving God. I also began to accept that it was okay I did not have other gifts. My leadership skills, my ability to write, my singing voice and any other talent I may have possessed were and are treasures. The fact that I can't ski, do math, play tennis or play the piano well are talents I was not given rather than failures. I began to believe in and accept the person I was created to be. I had much work to do to implement these new beliefs into my heart. But I had begun.

I do not think it was a coincidence that we met Haddon Robinson before we moved to Dallas. Vicki's gentle guidance through our friendship and the spiritual opportunities to which she led me combined with the seeking and praying I was practicing in the AA program of recovery resulted in the perfect work of the Master's hand. In light of the evidence in what followed, how can I believe otherwise?

The third major event that impacted us in 1986 was the founding of Adam's Camp. It was actually my mother's death that allowed this vision to become reality.

Diane, Adam's physical therapist, and I had been talking a great deal about the impact intensive therapy had on Adam's mobility. We were both sold on this model of treatment after Adam's great progress, and we realized this technique was seldom implemented and little known. At the same time, I reflected on the other needs we faced as a family. While Adam had great physical, occupational and speech therapists, the therapists did not communicate with each other. Their recommendations were good, but sometimes in conflict with another therapist's insights. Each therapist recommended we work with Adam for 45 minutes to an hour a day on their particular intervention. When did he have time to just play and when did I have time to fix dinner?

There was also the issue of connecting with other families raising kids with special needs. We never felt we had established any kind of a baseline in what to provide Adam because we didn't know much about what others were doing. We felt isolated, overwhelmed and inadequate.

Motivated by an interest in sharing the intensive therapy model with other families, we began to formulate an idea. Why not gather a few families together and provide a week of intensive therapy for their kids? Instead of just providing one type of therapy, wouldn't it be beneficial to include all the disciplines together? Our goals were to allow excellent therapists to work with our kids as a team so they could develop a comprehensive, individualized plan that would make sense for each child.

Then we thought, if a family was investing a week in their child, why not expand this idea to include an investment in the family? Find a location that would allow the families to stay in a recreational setting where respite and escape from everyday worries could refresh and refuel them. Diane had a connection with the director at Snow Mountain Ranch, the YMCA of the Rockies, near Winter Park, Colorado. The connection was a no brainer because of our shared mission of serving families and the perfect fit of their facility to our program. A great partnership was born.

In addition to offering our new program at a family-friendly facility, a Family Facilitator was brought on board to guide conversation between families to address feelings of isolation and offer them a network of new resources and ideas.

Once we had secured a location and Diane had identified four other families from her practice to participate, the dream took shape. Five families, five therapists, five days. This was the formula, and its implementation was missing only one important piece: seed money. When my mother passed in February, it seemed only natural to ask that memorials in her honor be contributed to this initiative. To honor her legacy, this dream was named Adam's Camp, after her grandson. I know my mom would have been so honored to know she played such a crucial role in this vision, and I experienced healing by honoring her in this way. Thanks to this small $1,200 legacy, four willing volunteers, five enthusiastic therapists and five eager families, a new channel of hope and healing was planted on a perfect mountainside under the clear Colorado skies. We had no idea what would happen that week nor what was to follow, but we felt the stirring of something special.

Three significant, seemingly unrelated events were all a part of 1986. A death that helped to spring new life. A move that brought a closer connection to God. And a dream that sprung out of a need. Seemingly unrelated, but all connected by the God who's timing and vision and creative ways of using broken people planted seeds of hope for our family, for others, and for me. The God I was finally coming to know.

14

A Pickup, Some Mats and Five Kids

DIANE, ADAM'S PHYSICAL therapist, was passionate about Adam's Camp, and she worked diligently with the therapists and volunteers to assemble and plan the details of that first week of Adam's Camp in early July of 1986. She hand-selected the best physical therapist, occupational therapists and speech therapist she knew to serve on the team. I use the term "serve" because while the intent was for the therapists to be paid through the client's insurance, all had agreed to take whatever reimbursement was available. These therapists were excited to participate in this unique experience where they could work side-by-side with their peers and create meaningful progress with these kids in a short period of time. While none of them had provided therapy in this multi-disciplinary way before, they could all see the value and potential of this model.

Meanwhile, I worked with the families to divvy up the responsibility for meals. We decided that each family would prepare one dinner during the week for the whole group.

One of the most remarkable components of camp was the partnership we began to build with Snow Mountain Ranch. We looked at this YMCA facility, located between Colorado's Winter Park and Granby, before we talked to Kent Meyer, the director, but did not consider or research any other properties as this one seemed to meet our needs.

I truly believe God orchestrated this partnership as it turned out to be the perfect fit for Adam's Camp for reasons that continued to be revealed as we grew. The most unique thing about the facility was the individual cabins available for the family and staff lodging. In addition, there were a number of activities offered at Snow Mountain Ranch that were perfect for our campers, and conference space available for therapy, all surrounded by some of the most breathtaking mountain scenery in all of Colorado.

Another interesting aspect of that first week was the diversity of our families, not ethnically, but structurally. We had two-parent, single-parent, and divorced-parent families represented in our little group of five. Yet the ties that bound us through raising our special children so easily overshadowed those differences. All our children were clients of Diane's, and all of us were there to provide an opportunity for our special children to grow and improve their functional skills.

Lisa was a six-year-old spunky blond who knew her mind and was willing to share it. Lisa had cerebral palsy like Adam and was there with her mom and dad who lived in Idaho Springs in the Colorado foothills. She had successfully begun to walk with braces on her legs and determination in her eyes. Her parents were hoping for improved movement and fine motor planning.

Joel also had cerebral palsy but was more highly impacted than either Adam or Lisa. He relied on a wheelchair for mobility and likely always would. Joel was non-verbal. His parents and sister came with him to camp. They were hoping to improve any functional skills Joel might develop such as sipping through a straw and managing his electric wheelchair.

Six-year-old Annie was funny and full of life. While her developmental disability was undiagnosed, it impacted her physically as well as mentally. Her parents were divorced, but both loved her and were there to support her. They were hoping she would improve her speech and movement.

Five-year-old Michael had spina bifada, a birth defect of the spine. He was bright and endearing and relied on a wheelchair as Joel did. Michael's single mom, who was hoping to see improvement in Michael's fine and gross motor skills, experienced the stress of single parenthood more than most in raising a child with special needs. We were reminded of that when she brought out her contribution to our group dinner – ten cans of Progresso Vegetable Soup. But we were grateful for her efforts, and all enjoyed every mouthful.

Rounding out the group was our six-year-old Adam. His quick wit and ready laugh folded well into the mix of our little group. Our goals for him were to improve his mobility as he continued to walk with assistance from his walker.

A month or so before that first session, we all gathered in the back yard of the house Diane used as her therapy space and office and had a picnic to meet the other families and to share our hopes and dreams for that week of camp with each other and the therapy staff. Our kids all had different diagnoses and our goals for our kids were very different. In every case, we sold ourselves short in our expectations of the outcomes from a week at Adam's Camp.

Weeks before arriving at camp, the therapists met a few times to discuss the goals for each child and the strategies they would use to address those goals. Each child would work one-on-one with a therapist for 30 to 40 minutes, then switch to another therapist until every child had worked with each therapist once a day. The therapy space was set up in a large conference room and consisted of some mats, balls and other equipment the therapists brought to use in treating kids during their sessions. Each therapist had their own area set up to facilitate the work they would be doing in their discipline that week.

The beauty of this model was that the quality of treatment was not dictated by the makeup of the group of kids. Each child had an individualized plan that was addressed one-on-one throughout the day with each therapist.

We didn't want to waste the opportunities provided in this outdoor setting, so built into the therapy day were typical camp activities that facilitated therapy. In these days before countless regulations, we created a solid therapy program utilizing some rather unorthodox strategies. The kids, therapists and parents spent time each afternoon participating in swim therapy in the Snow Mountain Ranch indoor swimming pool, serving as our own lifeguards. Once during the week, the therapists created their own version of therapeutic horseback riding by taking the kids on a trail ride on horses from the stables on grounds. Transport to and from activities for the kids and therapy team was in the back of Diane's small, worn pickup truck.

More orthodox were the snacks and lunch, which always included feeding therapy, teams often enjoyed on the picnic tables outdoors. In other words, from 8:30 in the morning until 4:30 in the afternoon, minus a two-hour break for rest in the afternoon, our kids were involved in therapy which, for them, often just seemed like fun.

Meanwhile, while our kids were in therapy, the families were free to do two things we rarely had the opportunity to enjoy. One was time alone with our spouse and, in ours and Joel's parents' case, with our other child. We were able to hike Snow Mountain and spend one-on-one time with Jared doing whatever he wanted to do. So much attention is devoted to a child with special needs, and the needs of other children in the family often shift to accommodate the special child.

The second opportunity we had was meeting and talking with other parents who shared this unique experience. We talked about our challenges in making the accommodations we had to make to provide our special kids a childhood rich in experience and development. Our fears and insecurities were laid out on the rough wood picnic table we gathered around each day. We commiserated with other parents who felt guilty about not doing enough therapy with their child, felt overwhelmed, and often angry and exhausted. We listened to what other families were doing to help their child, what resources they had discovered, and how they were finding time to take care of themselves.

We marveled at these great parents. Slowly we began to realize we were doing many of the same great things they were doing. We began to believe. We began to believe that we could do this. We began to believe our family was going to be okay, we were good parents offering strong support to Adam, and we were not alone. We began to believe there was hope.

After the therapy day was complete, the therapists took a well-deserved break, then we all met for dinner in the staff cabin at six. After enjoying the meal prepared by one of the families, laughing over the funny things that had happened during the day and marveling at the kids' accomplishments, we often piled the kids in wagons and took them on walks or to a small park near the staff cabin. We have photos of the sun setting behind the Indian Peaks as we all hiked to the top of the ridge to enjoy the spectacular view of the valley below. The majesty of the dazzling pink and orange sunset dwarfed our little group, but also served to illuminate the magic that was happening among us that week. We didn't know it at the time, but miracles would happen that first week at Adam's Camp.

I don't remember exactly what day it was, but at dinner one night toward the end of the camp week, therapists and families were all sitting around the living room of the main cabin as we did each night. We didn't think much about it at the time, but Adam was watching Lisa as she walked or, more accurately, lurched across the room, walking with great effort if not great form. A moment after Lisa reached her destination, Adam stood up and walked across the room by himself without a walker. I am not even sure he had a purpose. But he walked. Independently. For the first time in his life.

There were cheers and celebration all around. Bob and I were overwhelmed with joy and what I can only describe as wonder. Everyone was happy for Adam, and everyone was happy for us. Nowhere else could a group of people have better understood what this moment meant to us.

Tears flowed for many of us as we wondered together at the miracle that had just happened. What was it? What had been the catalyst to Adam walking right then? To this day, I couldn't tell you for sure. But after years of sharing similar experiences with other families, I believe there were a number of factors that came together to create that moment. I believe the therapy Adam had been receiving all week helped to prepare and strengthen his core to support him in taking these brave steps. I believe watching Lisa, who walked like *he* walked, helped him to believe in himself. I believe these families, gathered together for the sole purpose of helping our children for this one week, created an intangible space — an opening in our otherwise busy, distracted, pre-occupied lives — for such a moment as this.

While the families gathered our kids and returned to our rooms in the lodge for the night, the second part of the therapists' job was only beginning. They would go back to their cabin and begin the task of discussing each child, their challenges and accomplishments for the day. Each therapist in turn would offer their observations and make recommendations for the plan for that child the next day. By working together, they could see areas where their work might complement that of another therapist. They also could determine which therapies were most needed and how their work could contribute to the building of skills most emerging or most lacking in each child.

The therapists learned from each other and were able to experience the remarkable changes taking place with these kids in this intensive setting. Their typical style of working with kids once a week did not provide them with these type of results in such a short time, and it gave them new energy and confidence as they supported each other with this interdisciplinary work. It made them better therapists.

I still don't know where the therapists got the energy to work late into the night and show up ready to work with our kids the following day. I suspect they fed off the energy of each other, the results they were seeing and their passion for this work. Also, chocolate. Lots of chocolate. They were truly remarkable.

After the fifth day of therapy, the biggest challenge of the week awaited the therapists. The last night together, they created a comprehensive report for each child, presenting the results and recommendations they were offering to each family. The report included input from each therapist and was written in narrative form.

The next day, each family met with the therapy team for an hour to discuss the outcomes from the week. Bob and I met with the team and learned from each therapist their observations of Adam's strengths, his areas of growth during the week, and the challenges they suggested be addressed with his regular team of therapists going forward. We were given the report to share with his ongoing therapists so they could see what he had done, what he was capable of, and what strategies and interventions they recommended. That first year, this was a lengthy written report, but we learned that picture reports which demonstrated the intervention techniques and served as a visual memory book were much more useful to both parents and providers in future years.

I don't remember a lot of the specific moments of that first week, but I will never forget walking into the conference. We knew the therapists well and had developed great relationships with them, yet this was a whole new ballgame. We were about to hear their collective findings about our son. What would they say about his potential? Did they discover any glaring challenges we had missed? Did they like him?

. What we heard in that conference left us with a clearer vision of and for Adam. We learned he was capable of many things, and with the right intervention and practice, could acquire many independent skills. He could walk, which we discovered that week. He could perform such everyday skills as using a fork and spoon, locking and unlocking the front door, and putting his dishes in the dishwasher. We learned some of the adaptation techniques that would help Adam develop these skills and reach his full potential. We heard about the many extraordinary qualities he had including his speech and language. We saw how much he was loved as the therapists described our quirky, funny, wobbly, capable, whole son.

We walked into the conference with a vision of Adam divided into his physical, occupational, speech and behavioral needs and left the conference with a picture of our whole Adam. We left armed with techniques that were tailored to his specific needs and with confidence in those areas in which therapeutic intervention would be most helpful. We left with a tool to present to his teachers, doctors, therapists and caregivers that would allow them to be prepared in the same way we were now prepared. No longer would every provider have to figure Adam out before working with him. We had a document that clearly defined his abilities and his needs, and those working with him could start with a wealth of information it can take providers months to learn about a child without this roadmap.

On the last day of camp, we all gathered at the playground in the early morning to say goodbye and to celebrate what had been a phenomenal week for all of us. While not every family experienced the dramatic changes in their child that we did with Adam, every single child had accomplished a major breakthrough. The interaction with the other families had been empowering and healing for all of us, and I know we all left with greater confidence, a lighter heart, and renewed hope. Adam's Camp 1986 had been a success.

Adam's Camp gave Bob and me the emotional support, knowledge and faith to navigate the coming year of growth with our special family, including a new appreciation of Jared's special need to carve out his unique place in our family as the sibling of a special child.

Adam's Camp provided us with a new community of friends and fellow parents, all of us imperfect and committed to the well-being of our ever-evolving families while travelling a road we never dreamed we would be on … together. During the coming year, I would flash back to many of the things I learned or heard other parents share about their journey, and I would gather strength and wisdom from those parents.

Adam's Camp gave us a place to enjoy the pine-scented breath of healing; to stop just long enough to appreciate the majesty of the Indian Peaks and to realize that a God who could create all of this could surely provide our family all we could need or want. It gave us a chance to stop. To prioritize. To listen. Adam's Camp gave us hope. Adam's Camp gave us a new normal.

15

Wherever You Go, There You Are

IT SEEMED THE moving van headed for Dallas came before we had a chance to process the life-changing week we had just spent in the spectacular Rocky Mountains. It was exciting to share the good news about Adam walking with the neighbors and friends who had been a part of Adam's life since he was born, but we were soon to be separated from those dear friends by over 1,200 miles. I remember us all gathering at our house for one last neighborhood party before we would leave the next day.

By this time, I was coming to terms with my alcoholism, though not enough to actually quit drinking. I drank that night as we reminisced about the fun we had had over the seven years we were all together. I didn't want to leave and was not looking forward to living in Texas, but I shed no tears, as I was continuing to eat and drink down my feelings. I remember wondering why I wasn't more emotional. I was in another state of emotional lock down as we uprooted our family, our support system and what had become my early recovery network to begin a new chapter of our lives in Dallas.

I was what is commonly referred to as a "functional alcoholic." My life continued around me while I continued to anesthetize all the emotions that threatened to crack my strong exterior. I had not yet acknowledged to myself that I could not imagine my life without alcohol.

While at that time I would have said it was too much fun to give up, the truth was that I needed alcohol. I needed to have relief from the stresses of moving, from the challenges of raising two kids in a new town, and most of all from the constant voice in my head that kept telling me to binge and purge or drink. I only got drunk on the weekends, but my weeks were often peppered with binge-and-purge episodes which brought me similar relief. The calmness induced by these episodes was always followed by remorse. I was an addict, and my body and mind craved the peace and comfort my addictions could provide. There is a big difference between want and need, and it would take me awhile to accept that difference in myself.

We settled into a lovely home that had been decorated in the mauve and seafoam green colors popular in the eighties. The boys were enrolled in separate schools in our well-respected school district. The program for kids with special needs was at a school a few miles farther away than Jared's neighborhood school. Adam would be bussed to his school, and I spent a busy August meeting the boys' teachers and beginning the arduous task of establishing a network of providers for Adam. Looking for a pediatrician or pediatric dentist included expertise and experience serving kids with special needs as criteria, which narrowed the field considerably.

We met our next-door neighbors who had a daughter Jared and Adam's age and a younger son. Once school started, we began to meet other families from the neighborhood. There were couples from Bob's workplace we socialized with a bit, and we slowly began to find a rhythm to our new life in Texas.

If moving to Connecticut was a culture shock, moving to Dallas was a culture shock magnified by *bling*. Lots of it. There seemed to be no personal flaw or problem that couldn't be disguised by a designer outfit, lots of makeup and even more very bright, large jewelry. Fancy cars and homes decorated to excess were the norm here. It was clear that success, for many, was measured by the material in Dallas, and I knew I was a fish out of water the first time I went to the grocery store in my sweats sans makeup and was singled out for my ID in order to use my credit card. In time, I met many people in Dallas who do not fit this stereotype, but overall, I would say we usually felt way under-dressed for the ball.

We had access to a health club and a country club through Bob's work. I worked out at the health club where the boys enjoyed the other kids in childcare, which was great, but the country club was a bit of a misfit for our family. Lakewood Country Club was in the heart of Dallas, an old and established institution that catered to the Dallas gentry as far as I could tell. It was the only pool we could access for free, so I often took the kids there on stifling summer days to swim af-ter we went to the health club. On the heels of the familiar fun at our neighborhood pool in Homestead Farm in Denver, it was odd to be at this staid club with the boys, but few other kids. Jared remembers the diving board and the fruit bars we always purchased after swim time, but since all the neighborhood kids belonged to a different country club, the boys really had no friends at this pool. Neither did I. We were happy to have a place to swim, as Jared especially loved the water, but it was not the social opportunity we had hoped for. I felt disconnected and lonely.

While we never established a really close relationship with them, our next door neighbors, like us, enjoyed gourmet cooking and fine wine. We took turns entertaining and working to outdo each other with our elaborate meals, and the wine flowed freely. At first, I man-aged to drink somewhat moderately, but it wasn't long before my consumption reached levels I had come to rely on before I considered recovery. I only drank on the weekends, but I used those weekends to make up for the deprivation I experienced during the week, just as I had for years. Binging and purging always accompanied my drinking, so my behavior continued to mask how much I missed my friends and familiar surroundings.

My impression was that anything worth doing was worth doing in excess in Dallas, so it wasn't hard for me to nurture my addictions. It wasn't unusual for us to enjoy limo rides to the finest restaurants to enjoy great food and an abundance of champagne and wine compliments of the couple who owned the company Bob worked for. I was a party drinker, so this larger-than-life partying suited me just fine.

I don't really remember when I sought out Dallas AA, but I believe I was experiencing the same out-of-control feelings that brought me into those rooms in the first place. While on the outside, my life looked like all the other moms in our neighborhood, there was an emptiness and battle going on inside me most of the time. I felt shame because of my eating disorder and my alcoholism. I suffocated under a mountain of "shoulds." I should be happy because of my wonderful husband and kids. I should be grateful for my life and my health. I should be like other people who seem to be able to manage their lives without substances. I may not have understood the depth and breadth of alcoholism and addiction, but I did realize once again I needed help.

I tried a few different AA meetings and finally found a noon meeting about 10 minutes from our house that suited me. I attended meetings a few days a week, but I also continued to drink. In the meetings in Dallas, you always announced your sobriety date when you introduce yourself at the beginning of the meeting. At first, I would admit drinking and reset my sobriety date, but after a while I just fabricated a date and announced it at every meeting while I continued to drink.

One thing that seemed to move ahead in a positive way at that point was the igniting of my desire for a deeper relationship with God spearheaded by my new friend Vicki Hitzges. I had joined a Bible study she belonged to and Bob and I took the boys with us to church on Sundays. The duality of my life was magnified by my interest in spirituality while I once again felt ingenuous nursing a hangover while singing the words to "What a Friend We Have in Jesus." I realized my life better reflected what a friend I had in Chardonnay.

Once I began attending AA meetings again, the desire to stop drinking returned. I really felt, however, that I should give controlled drinking one more try. I decided I would drink one glass of wine a week. I truly do not know what I thought this would accomplish. Never in my life was I satisfied with one glass of wine. The only thing I knew for sure would happen if I had one glass of wine was that I would want another glass of wine. Yet for some strange reason, I decided the solution to my alcoholic dilemma was to prove I could actually control this. I could still experience the ease and comfort of that first drink like normal people could. I could train myself to become a normal drinker.

For the next year or so, I managed to drink one glass of wine on Saturday night. I enjoyed it. I put lots of ice in the glass to stretch it out. I anticipated that glass of wine all week. I thought about what kind of wine I would have. Then I forced myself not to refill the glass, although the glass did seem to be getting larger. Eventually, one glass became two, and not long after that, I lost count of how many glasses of wine I was drinking. That experiment is one of the craziest things I have ever done. It was testimony to how desperately I was clinging to my control. I just could not admit I was truly powerless over alcohol.

At the same time, I was making an effort to become involved in the community. I transferred my Junior League Membership from Denver to the Richardson Junior League. Richardson is a suburb north of Dallas that doesn't carry the weight of power and prestige as Dallas – I knew I wasn't ready for that. I met some nice women there and began to get involved in service work. I volunteered in the boys' classrooms and was co-leader of the cub scout troop to which Adam and Jared belonged. We became accustomed to saying the pledge of allegiance to the Texas flag after the pledge to the American flag at school events even though we felt like we existed in some parallel universe while doing so.

Jared made friends with some of the kids in the neighborhood and seemed to find his place. But many of my fondest memories about Dallas revolve around Adam. Little Adam rode a BIG bus to school, and he loved greeting Stanley the bus driver every morning when he arrived. Stanley and Adam had a truly special relationship. Stanley would tease Adam about something every day, and Adam's contagious laugh would set the tone for his ride to school and for my day. We hired sweet Fanny to come and clean and watch the boys once a month. I would pick Fanny up and she would always be excited to see the boys. The sweet relationship she had with them overshadowed her tendency to leave our dining room furniture sticky with <u>way</u> too much furniture polish.

Charlotte was one of the of the volunteers I served with in Junior League. Her Junior League volunteer placement was with a program that provided summer activities for kids with special needs, and Adam became a part of that program. Charlotte fell in love with Adam, and she and her family would often come and get Adam to take him for ice cream or on an outing with her clan. Adam remembers her fondly to this day.

Adam's team of preschool teachers were so special and quickly clued into Adam's sense of humor. They often took field trips and frequently went to teacher Miss Burleson's house to fix lunch and learn domestic skills, so they had met her husband Buster. One day she was sick after a field trip, and Adam welcomed her return by saying: "Did you and Buster have a good time in bed last night?" One of *many* Adamisms over the years.

Adam brought the best people into our lives no matter where we went. Everyone loved Adam. They loved both our boys, but because of his special needs, Adam brought people together in an extraordinary way. It's as if the purity of his spirit broke all barriers and allowed us to connect with a place in our own hearts that often lays dormant. If others could circumvent pity when they experienced Adam, they discovered authenticity. Unencumbered by the conventions of human behavior we so dutifully teach our neuro-typical kids, we looked into eyes that reflected only Adam's raw and beautiful truth. There was no pretense. There was only joy and love, a little mischief and more often than not, a completely inappropriate comment or two. Adam was the real deal.

16

If at First You Don't Succeed...

THE FOLLOWING SUMMER, returning to Dallas after camp was less difficult than it had been the year before, now that we had established some connection with neighbors and friends from Bob's company. Jared had friends in the neighborhood and Adam was included enough to keep him happy. Both boys adapted to the hot, humid summer days in Texas and attended a day camp through the YMCA for a few weeks, but aside from that, outdoor activity in the summer was limited to swimming at the country club.

Our second full year in Dallas kicked off with the beginning of school in August of 1987. Jared began first grade at Moss Haven Elementary while Adam continued to attend Lake Highlands, the local school with classrooms for kids with special needs.

My routine of working out, attending Bible Study or meetings with Junior League, working in the kids' classrooms, or helping with Boy Scouts and frequenting the Dallas malls kept me busy during the week. I was usually involved in planning for weekend get-togethers with neighbors as well.

I continued attending AA meetings, though I was certainly not sober. My sobriety was intermittent at best. No matter my resolve, I could not keep myself from stopping at the liquor store on Friday afternoons. I was pretending to be sober in AA while continuing to try to control my drinking. Still convinced that I was different from most alcoholics and that my disease was indeed manageable, I sought yet another way to control my drinking. I decided my experiment drinking one glass of wine a week could rationally be considered "sobriety." I thought I could use AA to manage my drinking in spite of all the recommendations and evidence to the contrary. In retrospect, my need to control my life was epic. I preferred the agony of wrestling with demon alcohol to the idea of actually surrendering my will to a proven solution.

For an alcoholic, taking one drink and stopping is far greater torture than not drinking at all. What differentiates an alcoholic from the normal drinker is the phenomenon of craving. Once an alcoholic takes a drink, that craving sets in and the thought that takes over is more. More alcohol.

I thought about that glass of wine I was going to have on the weekend all week, and after drinking it, had to continue fighting the urge to drink more. As I watched others refill their wine glasses, I would count the minutes until we could finally sit down and eat dinner. The cocktail hour seemed to last forever as I nursed that one glass of wine. I viewed that wine as a "reward" for my week of abstinence, yet the comfort or enjoyment of the drink only set up a desire for more. The Big Book of Alcoholics Anonymous described my dilemma perfectly when it said: "For most normal folks, drinking means release from care, boredom and worry. It means joyous intimacy with friends and a feeling that life is good. But not so with us...The old pleasures were gone. There was an insistent yearning to enjoy life as we once did, and a heartbreaking delusion the some new miracle of control would enable us to do it. There was always one more attempt – and one more failure."

I finally realized my experiment at controlled drinking was failing to make me into a normal drinker. What I was doing wasn't working. The gig was up. I knew my only hope at peace and healing was to get completely sober and the only way I was going to be able to do that was to get completely honest.

In April of that year, I walked into an AA meeting and admitted to the group I had been lying about my sobriety date and had been drinking all along. I was sure the room would come to a shocked standstill, but instead I was met with encouragement and was told to "keep coming back." I realized my lies had only been hurting me, and that others in the room, while supportive, were really not focused on *my* sobriety as they were busy working on their own. Who knew? That was effectively my first real act of surrender.

The next change I succumbed to was to get a sponsor and actually do what she told me to do. I had come into this program believing the 12 steps of Alcoholics Anonymous were fine for those who were in need of all 12, but I could probably get by with five or six of them. I didn't have a sponsor as I was not sure I could trust anyone to agree with my plan of action and rejected the idea that someone else might know how to do this deal better than I did. I was arrogant and far from humble, until I realized I could not quit drinking.

Deana was a little older than I and had been sober for a long time. She was married to a recovering alcoholic she had met in AA, and she truly walked the talk. I respected her, asked her to be my sponsor, and became entirely ready to do whatever she asked me to do, whether I thought it would help me or not. I met with her every week and we read the Big Book, essentially the instruction manual of Alcoholics Anonymous, together. I knew this program was based on spiritual principles, and while I admired those who seemed to rely on their relationship with a higher power to keep them sober, I doubted my ability to connect with the power I called God at that level. I was continuing to seek God through AA, church and bible study, but I told my sponsor I believed I was too controlling and strong-willed to allow God to take control of my life. My ability to trust was damaged. Her only response was: "Do you believe that I believe?" I did. I truly did believe Deana had that kind of relationship with God. She told me that would be enough for now. And it was. I remained sober for three months.

17

Adam's Camp Revisited...

IN THE SUMMER of 1988, we returned for our third summer of Adam's Camp. Diane had once again assembled a great team of therapists and organized the program details. Since I was living in Dallas, Diane assumed oversight of the entire program which was easier now that the formula was in place. I will forever be grateful for her leadership those first years.

The families involved were committed for another year, and four new families joined to make a total of 15 families for the week. As with the two years prior, each family and child brought their goals and hopes to the beautiful Frasier Valley and laid them at the feet of the talented therapy staff, the social worker and each other. Once again, Adam's Camp filled our cup. Adam thrived and we enjoyed the fellowship and support of the phenomenal parents and staff who came together to create this magic. We marveled at the progress we saw through the therapy, especially in the kids new to Adam's Camp. We celebrated the changes in the new parents as they came to realize, as we had that first year, that their family may not be "normal" by the world's interpretation, but it was special and perfect in its own right. We laughed out loud often while tears of empathy and joy were never far removed from any conversation.

That summer a program was introduced at Snow Mountain Ranch

that became an integral part of Adam's Camp: Therapeutic Horseback Riding. A woman with a passion for providing the proven benefits of hippotherapy- horseback riding as therapy- to our kids with special needs had opened a center on site, and our program was a perfect fit. Each child was able to ride at least once during their week of camp, and this intervention became a highlight for many of them. Hippotherapy helped our kids with balance, other types of movement and overcoming fears. The kids were able to groom and feed the horses and came to have their favorites. Adam was especially fond of a sweet brown and white mottled horse named Minute, and Adam and Minute became fast friends.

Any notion we may have had that Adam's Camp would become stale or redundant after a few years was alleviated that summer. The support and therapy were as helpful and useful as it had ever been as we again took the results of the week back to Dallas to share with Adam's ongoing therapists, school and medical providers. That second year, Adam returned from camp more confident and willing to try new things. He gained strength through the therapy and was able to walk more steadily. Adam's mobility always improved at camp, and we came to learn far more about what he *could* do than what he couldn't do while we were there. Recognizing potential and developing strengths was always the point of Adam's Camp, and we encouraged others to expect no less from Adam as he moved through school and social settings.

By now, we knew Adam's Camp was far more than a program. Adam's Camp was a family. With the usual daily cares of our world left behind for this one week, we sank into the strong and loving arms of Adam's Camp. Driving down the mile-long tree-lined entrance to Snow Mountain Ranch gave us just enough time to transition from the four-lane-highway life we were used to into the still beauty that would nurture our minds, bodies and souls for the week.

God's hand in Adam's Camp was served up in abundance every day at Snow Mountain Ranch. Every evening, just when it looked like the sun was going to sink unnoticed behind the Indian Peaks, a wash of orange, red and pink would caress the mountaintops and fill the sky with jaw-dropping glory. The waterfall hike introduced a variety of wildflowers, some bold and brilliant, others delicate and pale, as they paved the way to the cool and welcoming falls that served as a reward at the end of the winding trail. The night sky was brilliant with stars undisguised by the glare of city lights. And in the quiet mornings, I could swear I heard the voice of God whispering through the strong pines and the gentle Aspen as I sat on the porch with my coffee and my thoughts.

It may have been the idea of a few people that created the program of Adam's Camp. But no human entity could possibly have created the healing beauty and peace that surrounded us as we went about the business of serving our kids and families. Because it is impossible to measure the value of this setting on the entire experience for families, I have come to believe that God blessed Adam's Camp from the very beginning. He inspired the idea of bringing families together because God is all about relationship. He led us to Snow Mountain Ranch and knew the perfect formula was now in place. In the years following, Snow Mountain Ranch and the community surrounding it have provided Adam's Camp far greater gifts than we ever could have imagined. All the intangibles that make Adam's Camp valuable to each family are only fully realized in the eyes of the One who created it. No human power could have seen this coming.

The clarity I was experiencing that summer came as a result of my new-found sobriety. As I continued my work with Deana and began to take life one day at a time, I settled into the practice of the first three steps of AA:

1. I admitted I was powerless over alcohol and my life had become unmanageable.
2. Came to believe that a power greater than myself could restore me to sanity.
3. Made a decision to turn my will and my life over to the care of a power greater than myself, seeking only knowledge of his will for me and the power to carry it out.

The operative word here is "practice." I was still a ways from truly admitting my unmanageability or turning my life and will fully over to God, but I had a true desire to embrace this way of life. In AA, the keys to true healing begin with HOW (honesty, open mindedness, and willingness) and I had embraced all of these concepts. I had become honest with my AA group about my struggle and my sobriety, I was far more openminded about the value of all 12 steps of the program, and I was willing to do what my sponsor asked me to do. The results of this change in my attitude allowed me to not drink, one day at a time. It reminded me of the parable about the mustard seed in the bible. It only takes a start to launch the beginning of a completely different way of living.

Through newly sober eyes, I found countless expressions of joy and beauty previously veiled behind my anxious need to control my emotions and environment. We had experienced so many miracles at Adam's Camp the first two years, but that year revealed a glimpse of the depth and weight of this experience.

Have you ever had Lava Cake? It is a small chocolate cake, usually accompanied by either whipped cream or ice cream. It looks incredibly delicious, and when you take that first bite, you are met with the rich chocolate cake you were anticipating . You may sit back and savor that bite, thinking you have found the perfect dessert – especially if you are a chocolate lover like I am. But when you dig into that second bite, you discover that you had barely skimmed the potential of this culinary adventure. Your spoon meets a warm, rich, even more chocolatey center that delivers an aroma and flavor that eclipses that of the cake with astonishing authority. You realize that, had you stopped at that first bite, you would have missed the core splendor of this creation. It leaves you anxious to combine a bite of the cake with ice cream and newfound lava to see what new delight awaits your tongue.

That is how I felt about the entire Adam's Camp experience that year, especially the natural beauty surrounding us. I had seen it but delving into the center of all Adam's Camp is required me to be fully present. I began to develop a knowing. A knowing this God I was turning my life over to was crafting a remarkable oasis, all clad in spectacular beauty, hope and familial love. A knowing that God used me, wounded and so imperfect, to help Him bring this delicious creation to life. A knowing that He was, is and ever will be the warm, rich, magic-producing center of Adam's Camp. Even though Adam's Camp is not a program openly acknowledging spirituality, I had a knowing. I have that knowing more than ever today.

While my sobriety did not last through that summer, I have never lost the knowing.

18

Family Disease Number 2

WE RETURNED TO Dallas after that third summer of camp with renewed commitment to move back to Colorado for good. We missed the outdoors and the laid-back culture we loved, not to mention our friends.

I don't remember exactly when I noticed the lump in my right breast, but I did report it to my doctor who suggested we "keep an eye on it." The lump was small and despite my recent experience with my mother's breast cancer, I wasn't particularily alarmed. Six months later, the doctor ordered a biopsy of the lump that was still there.

A friend from our neighborhood drove me to the biopsy appointment at the end of June. I still remember being sedated but conscious when the pathologist, who was in the room with the doctor when he performed the procedure, declared the lump was indeed malignant. What? Did I hear that right? Did the pathologist realize that he was delivering that news to ME at the same time he was telling the doctor? Did he have any idea I was conscious?

My eyes filled with tears as the doctor realized what had happened. It was the first indicator of a doctor less equipped to deal with a breast cancer diagnosis than other doctors who specialize in this area. All I knew was I had now become a statistic who would deal with the same disease that had killed my mother not two years earlier. My life had taken a dramatic turn from focus on the disease of alcoholism that killed my father to the disease of breast cancer that killed my mother. At 38-years-old, I was a double winner, battling two family diseases at once. It didn't take me long to decide I could only deal with one thing at a time, and breast cancer won out.

True to my nature, I sprang into action. I researched cancer treatment in Dallas and made the decision to see Dr. George Peters at Baylor Medical Center. He had a stellar reputation and practiced at the highly revered hospital operated by Baylor University. The diagnosis came just before July 4th weekend, so I had to wait several days for an appointment. Waiting is not my specialty, and the days over that weekend were long and difficult.

Dr. Peters was kind, knowledgeable and straightforward. I trusted him and was relieved to hear that the tumor was small and very treatable, even in 1988. However, the doctor who had originally biopsied my tumor did not complete the needed testing of the tumor before disposing of it. The course of treatment would have typically been determined by whether the tumor was an estrogen receptor or not. That was unknown. Watching my mom suffer with a cancer that eventually metastasized to her bones causing a slow, painful death made my decision easy. I chose the most aggressive form of treatment: a mastectomy followed by chemotherapy. Let the games begin.

The surgery wasn't terrible, but I think I was in the hospital for about five days. During that time and after I returned home, neighbors and friends brought food and helped out with the boys. After a brief recovery, I began chemotherapy.

Sometimes friends took me for treatment and other times I drove myself. The treatments took several hours, and I remember staring at the tube pumping the toxic poison into my arm wondering "is the treatment more lethal than the disease?" I was certainly nauseous after those treatments, and even the smell of many foods made me sick. I remember the day I stood in the shower and caught my thick dark hair in handfuls as it fell from my head. I was prepared for losing my hair, but seeing my bald head in the mirror brought the reality of my cancer into full focus. I had two wigs. At home, I wore a bandana. I still went to my aerobics class in my bandana and went about my normal business as a mom. It was life as usual, only bald and with cancer.

By now, you can probably guess where I buried the emotion and stress surrounding this traumatic turn of events. Booze and food were my go-to buddies once again. Chemo dampened my enjoyment of both substances, but it didn't stop me from indulging. Food and booze created a familiar port in the storm, and while I did pray for strength, courage and healing, God didn't provide the quick fix I had relied on for so many years through alcohol and food.

Many people were kind to us during this time, but I was acutely aware of my loneliness and the distance between myself and my dearest friends. A few of them even offered to come and help out, which I declined. Bob's parents offered to come, which I also declined. I didn't want to deal with having anyone else in our home. Bob did his best to juggle his job and the help he was providing with the kids when he was home. I appreciated those who brought meals except for the sweet friend who brought pork chops in tomatoes and peppers. That may have been the all-time number one nausea-inducer. I will never forget that smell.

Then came the reconstructive surgery. I had very small breasts. I was told by the plastic surgeon that he had inserted both the smallest implant he had ever used (mine) and the largest one (someone else I can only imagine) in the same day. I emerged pretty lopsided and beat up in an area I had never viewed as a strength to begin with. Combined with my bald head, let's just say my days as runner-up to Miss University of Northern Colorado seemed far behind me. Breast cancer stripped me of my femininity in the most brutal ways. My appearance was important to me, and the loss of two major female attributes was jarring. I tried to avoid the mirror whenever possible, especially when I was wigless.

The saving grace about this experience was that I knew it would end. I was confident the treatment would be successful since the tumor was small. The chemo was certainly a challenge, but I emerged with a great prognosis. I was grateful for that. After chemotherapy was over, I began to grow my hair and soon sported a short hairdo for the first time in many years. More importantly, I recommitted myself to recovery from family disease number one – alcoholism.

The boys weathered my cancer treatment well and were young enough to easily accept I would get better and everything would be fine. After school began in August, the year continued without further incident, if you don't count the poor treatment Jared received from a second-grade teacher who didn't particularly like boys. She put masking tape around his desk to indicate the space he had in which to move about, as if this imaginary "cage" would enclose his silly behavior and inappropriate talking in class. I am not saying Jared didn't deserve some sort of discipline, but this was punitive and ineffective. She admitted she preferred girls, and I acknowledged (not to her) that I preferred other teachers. Jared doesn't really remember this experience, so I am happy to say this treatment didn't lead to years of therapy, but it sure did make *me* unhappy.

We were always mindful of ensuring Jared didn't feel like the second wheel to Adam. Jared was special in his own way. He was definitely on the fringe when it came to the typical interests of eight-year-old boys. While he was willing to give sports a try, his interest was marginal. That became glaringly evident when he played soccer and spent most of his time on the field talking to the players from the other team. He played t-ball and we spent many hot summer afternoons watching him enjoy the popsicles at the end of the game more than playing the game.

Eventually, Jared's friends and activities began to align more with his interests. He and Adam both liked participating in the Cub Scout Troop in which I served as a Den Mother. But more than anything else, Jared liked to create. Even at eight, he was an emerging writer. In the school talent show, he wrote and performed an original poem.

A Pirate Poem

I'm the sole survivor
Of when our ship sank-
Say one dirty word about me
And you'll walk the plank!

We are bad pirates
And we all have a sharpened sword-
But I'm the only pirate left

(And believe me, I get bored!)

I miss the good old days
When we fought battles on the ship-
I remember fighting Long John Silver
And I gave him a bloody lip!

The reason I have this eye patch on
Is because of when
The captain cut me in the eye
And so, did his rotten men.

But I stand on this sunny island
With lots and lots of pleasure
Because no one will ever find
My secret buried treasure

Well, it's bye-bye from Jared
The famous pirate, as you have heard
(And about the buried treasure,
Don't say a SINGLE WORD)

Well, I've had enough of this pirate stuff
I think I will go back
Oh my gosh, I'm still on stage!
I'm ruining my act!

Jared liked to draw and paint and participate in anything imaginary. The foreshadowing of this talent came when he was in pre-school. His teacher called Bob and I in for a conference at which we were prepared to hear about his need to better manage his behavior, but instead were told that Jared had a creative mind that was one in 10,000. We had two very special kids.

Dallas had a strong cultural scene, and we had subscriptions to two different children's theaters. We often attended cultural fairs both boys enjoyed, and Jared even fancied himself a magician for a time. His mind was active and clever, and we were always entertained by his humor.

We talked openly with Jared about how he felt about having a brother with special needs and another brother who died shortly after birth. There was and still is much talk about "survivor's guilt" in the world of special needs, and we wanted to help Jared identify and be okay with the guilt if it did exist in him. He continued to insist he did not have those feelings, though they have popped up from time to time since then. Jared seemed happy and healthy, though he did bite his nails down to the quick from an early age. While I tried not to put too much weight on that, this was one of the early signs foreshadowing the presence of a genetic trait I wish he had not inherited.

I reclaimed my sobriety after a four-month hiatus, , determined to pick up where I left off before my cancer diagnosis. Deana, my sponsor, and I began working the steps in earnest in October. I stayed sober for another three months, working the steps, going to meetings and praying, throughout the holidays and all the way to my 40th birthday celebration in January.

Bob was out of town on business for my birthday. His boss, Sharon, decided to compensate for his absence by taking me and a few other gals from Bob's office out on the town for this big milestone celebration. She picked us all up in a limo, and we went to the finest restaurant in Dallas for dinner. The champagne flowed the minute I set foot in that limo, and I knew I was going to drink it. I drank the champagne, then wine all through dinner, and drinks afterward. Oddly, the celebration was a letdown. It was glamorous and featured all the components of a BIG life, but the drunker I got, the more I knew that this was not for me. I felt empty and inauthentic and just plain inebriated without any of the joyful, fabricated high I used to rely on.

The next day, I went to an AA meeting and announced my relapse. I knew that I was done drinking. I felt it down to the core of my being. Alcohol was no longer working for me, and I was tired of fighting it. I was just ... done.

Finally, I could imagine my life without alcohol. I could imagine a life where I could find joy in the moment and peace with God. I could see a future that included less drama and more acceptance of myself and the life I had been given. I felt the presence of God beginning to fill the hole I had so carefully reserved for alcohol. I believed the message of recovery, and I surrounded myself with the people who were living the life I was seeking. I drew strength from them as I continued to be led into this life of freedom and faith. I had hope.

19

Home Again, Home Again, Jigitly Jig

WHENEVER WE PULLED into the garage or walked in the front door of our house, it became a habit for us to say, "Home again, home again, jiggity jig." It's a line from the rhyme,

> *"To market, to market, to buy a fat pig,*
> *Home again, home again, jiggity jig"*

That rhyme took on new meaning for us in the spring of 1989 when Bob went to the owners of the small company he worked for to ask them permission to move back to Colorado. Bob was travelling a lot anyway, and if he were to spend a few nights a week in Dallas, he was certain he could do his job.

The thing that dampened Bob's spirit most about Dallas was the lack of access to the great outdoors he had come to love in Colorado. If we were to get in our car and drive two hours from Dallas in any direction to escape city life for a weekend, we would end up in the middle of nowhere. There were no mountains, and while there were some lakes nearby, they lacked the beauty and solace of our magnificent Rockies. We missed our friends in Denver and knew we were not going to be in Dallas for the long haul. Between the two of us, we decided it was time to go home.

By the grace of God, Bob's company agreed to his request to move back to Denver and continue his work from there. It didn't take us long to put our house on the market, find a new house in Denver and plan for a move that would have us settled by the time the school year started. We found a home in the Cherry Creek School District about ten miles east of where we had lived before we moved to Dallas.

Our packing became lighter after some fellows robbed our house in broad daylight a few days before the school year ended. It appeared I may have walked in on them as there were things left that seemed they would have been taken based on what else they stole. They helped themselves to all our electronics--televisions, computers, my guitar, and all of Bob's clothes. The only thing we can figure is that one of them was Bob's size and had great taste in men's suits. It turned out our insurance covered these items, so we didn't have to pay to move them and were able to purchase all new electronics and clothes for Bob when we arrived in Denver. How's that for looking at the glass half-full?

When we crossed the Colorado state line on our drive back to Denver, Bob got out of the car and kissed the ground. We were so relieved and grateful to be home. Our new home was a little farther east that we had hoped, but the view of the mountains from the kitchen windows, and the 1.25 acres of land were irresistible. Our house was in the school district we wanted to be a part of which influenced our decision as well.

Creekside Elementary became the home school for both boys; Adam began the year in second grade and Jared in third. I was impressed with the special education team and was happy that Adam would be included in the regular classroom with support from an occupational therapist and a speech therapist once a week.

We re-established with our pediatricians at Partners in Pediatrics who had become much more than our doctors over the past year, even in our absence. Before we moved to Dallas, I had talked with the team at Partners in Pediatrics (or PIP as they were called) about Adam's Camp and the magic that had happened for us and others that first summer.

Jerry Rubin, Dean Prina and Jordan Klein were building a flourishing practice and decided to host a festive, family-friendly concert to encourage a feeling of community with their clients. While celebrating their practice, they chose to benefit the larger community by making the event a fundraiser. Adam's Camp was privileged to be named the recipient of the $2,000 raised that year, which represented our first donation and began a partnership that still exists today. It was a gift to be taken into the PIP family with our shared vision of stronger families which made this partnership a perfect fit.

Since we knew Denver well, it didn't take us long to plug back in. Our neighborhood was full of kids, including many boys around Jared and Adam's age. We had a neighborhood pool which became the scene of many a cannon ball and belly flop contest and lots of wide-open space for Jared to run and bike with friends. Jared joined the swim team which he truly enjoyed and many a Saturday was spent cheering him on at swim meets. This was more like it.

Though we were unable to attend Adam's Camp that year due to our move, I could hardly wait to jump back into camp planning and the development of the organization with both feet. We realized that in order to raise money to help support any future camps, we would need to secure non-profit status. One of the requirements for non-profit status was a board of directors, so Diane and I came up with a few people who functioned in name only at that point, with the exception of Diane who worked hard to complete the paperwork necessary to acquire this non-profit designation.

When I think back on those very early years, I can honestly say I had no vision of what Adam's Camp would become. I just knew we needed help if we were going to move forward with even one more year of camp. We needed to build and utilize a board of directors to help with the many tasks associated with running and organizing camp. Our contacts in the community allowed us to pull together a group of like-minded supporters and we began the task of strengthening the foundation of Adam's Camp.

The newly constructed board consisted of an accountant who

had a sister with Down syndrome, an attorney, the mom of a child with Down syndrome still too young for camp, a pediatric dentist who worked with a number of kids with special needs, a marketing professional with a heart for helping the community, the consultant who helped PIP put together their special event, Diane Aiken (now Legner) and me. The combination of experience and expertise on this board allowed us to begin writing our mission statement, by-laws, articles of incorporation, budget and other documents that solidified our framework and clarified our mission. Until we took this step, we had never dreamed far enough ahead to see a future for Adam's Camp, let alone the potential of what it was to become.

In our discussions about the uniqueness of intensive therapy, the board was sold on the powerful progress this type of intervention facilitated in kids with developmental disabilities. After witnessing the impact it had had on Adam and others in those first years of camp, we acknowledged that this intervention might be even more effective for children younger than six. Early intervention was known to be critical for children from birth to five years old. Our board didn't take long to start dreaming, and our first order of business in expanding our programs was finding a way to serve kids younger than five.

The limiting factor of the Adam's Camp model for younger children was the length of the therapy day. Younger children nap, so an all-day program would not work for them. However, a program that provided three hours of therapy a day for five consecutive days could adapt this model to younger children in a modified way. With this in mind, our Early Start program was born.

The first session of Early Start was held in the fall of 1989. Since this was a day program that did not involve lodging or meals it was much easier to organize logistically. The team was made up of five children and five therapists and was held in the offices of a physical therapist Diane knew. The therapy was successful, and bringing together those families also provided the sense of community and support found in our mountain camps. All the kids made gains that week which confirmed our notion that intensive therapy was valuable at as early an age as possible. We saw the same hope and strength dawn in the parents who participated that week as we did in our mountain therapy families.

With this first session of Early Start, we had successfully launched our second program.

20

Our New Normal

THE COMING YEARS of my life in sobriety were filled with what our family had come to view as normal. Without the chaos and internal struggle of alcohol in my life, I was able to participate more fully with my kids and Bob. I attended AA meetings in Denver, got a sponsor, and continued to do the work required to maintain the joy and freedom I had come to treasure. A new feeling was introduced into my life as I continued to pray and follow the spiritual path laid before me in my program of recovery. I finally had peace.

After visiting several churches, we found one that nourished our faith and also had a great children's ministry. I jumped back into Junior League of Denver, was active helping at the kids' school and we joined an athletic club. Bob was travelling quite a bit as a remote employee, so holding down the fort was my primary role in those years. Many of the other moms in the neighborhood also had travelling husbands, so we got together often.

My life as a typical stay-at-home mom was now filled with many of the same challenges and joys experienced by my friends and neighbors. I loved being home with my kids, but I have to say my work with Adam's Camp gave me an added sense of purpose. I know I was blessed to have a husband who worked hard and made it possible for me to stay home, and that gift allowed me the time to follow my pull to contribute to the world. Today, I view that desire to make a difference as a gift from God, but more on that later. With alcohol no longer a driving force in my life, my energy became more focused on what I believe I was created to do. I still battled bulimia, but my binging episodes were far fewer and farther between.

As with any fledgling non-profit, Adam's Camp's greatest need was money. In addition to creating the documents we needed to provide structure to the organization, our board's first project was to support the efforts of PIP (Partners in Pediatrics) in organizing their family concert for the following year. The artist they selected to perform was Linda Arnold, a well-known children's singer from California who had several recordings and a strong following. The Denver Center for the Performing Arts was the perfect venue to draw families throughout the Denver Metro Area. I pulled together a committee of friends and Adam's Camp supporters and ventured into the arena of event planning. I had always been an organizer, so some of these skills came naturally, while others I learned by trial and error.

The concert was well received. We marketed the event citywide, and over 1200 people attended. Our timing was good as Denver was starved for quality children's entertainment in those days. We raised $5,000 which was more than twice as much as the year before. In 1990, $5,000 went much further than it does today, and Adam's Camp was able to purchase its own mats and some equipment as well as offer a few scholarships.

21

Soul Changing

THE WORK TO support Adam's Camp intensified my passion for the organization, but our family didn't attend camp that year. Adam was doing well and had outgrown the traditional therapy the program offered.

But Ben Wharton did attend. Ben and his fellow campers provided us with more than enough motivation to continue our efforts to keep Adam's Camp alive and well for that next deserving family.

Ben had a rare developmental disorder characterized by low cognitive, nonverbal presence. Ben started attending Adam's Camp when he was four years old. Adam's Camp became one of the greatest joys of his life, and the most significant event of his year according to his mom, Jan. Over the course of his lifetime, Ben attended over 25 sessions of Adam's Camp. After every session, his parents were amazed at how Ben developed new skills, new vocabulary, new songs, new friends, and best of all, new confidence. He was much braver at camp than he ever was at home.

Sadly, Ben died in his late 20's. From early in Adam's Camp's infancy, Ben and his parents became a strong and vibrant thread in the rich tapestry of unique, precious families who became a part of the larger Adam's Camp family. Everyone loved Ben, knew Ben, and celebrated Ben for who he was. His endless choruses of "It's a Small World," his obsession with Kermit the frog, his love of The Beatles and his joy for all things Adam's Camp have become legend. His story lives on through so many of us who knew him.

Watching Ben and many other families experience what our family had at Adam's Camp fueled our passion and encouraged the board members, therapists and volunteers in our work. I walked away from every Adam's Camp meeting or visiting any session with a full cup. Hope is contagious. Adam's Camp was so rich with tender personal stories of progress and hope, it was impossible not to be drawn into the Adam's Camp Magic, as it came to be known. Everyone we told about camp, whether they had a personal connection to the world of disabilities or not, saw the impactful results of the program.

In most narratives, this would be the part where I talk about Adam's Camp being life changing. That term has become painfully overused in the non-profit world. At Adam's Camp, if a child learns to walk like Adam did, that is definitely life changing. If a child learns to speak, that is also life changing. All of that is incredibly important, don't get me wrong. But I believe Adam's Camp is so much more than life changing. Adam's Camp is soul changing.

Year after year, I watched the tired and discouraged faces of our parents as they walked through the doors to check-in for camp. They had loaded the car with a week's worth of provisions, including all the extra things needed for their special child. They had navigated a long drive, dealing with potential physical or emotional needs over and above those of the typical child. They often showed up tired and looking almost apologetic as they juggled the logistics of checking in while managing the behavior of their special child and siblings. .

I always worked the check-in table that first day of each session. Greeting these families with love as we finally put a face to folks we had been talking with over the phone for months was one of the greatest joys of this work for me. We acknowledged each of their kids equally, and most of all offered these parents a knowing embrace to let them know...we get it.

After welcoming the families with a gift bag including things like games for the kids, a first aid kit, a flashlight (it was VERY dark at night), some snacks and other fun camp-related things, we described the schedule for the rest of the day. A wine and cheese reception at 6:30 would be their first chance to meet the other parents and their therapy team that evening. We would encourage them to check into their cabins, unpack and decompress for an hour or so before dropping their kids off at childcare and joining the other families. Usually, we saw them start to relax, recognizing they were among their people, much like we did our first year at camp.

The wine and cheese gathering was like bringing together a group of old friends for the first time. The parents had been talking on the phone with the program director at Adam's Camp to discuss team placement, finances and logistics for their child for months prior to camp. In addition to filling out extensive paperwork, parents had talked to a therapist from their team about their special child, allowing the team to be prepared to address the goals for the child that week on day one. On this night, the exhaustive application process, screening, completion of paperwork, scholarship considerations and payment plans were finished. It was time for face-to-face conversations with people you may have never met, but feel you know already.

Gisela, our camp cook for many years, was especially proud of her chocolate-covered strawberries. These always held center stage on the table ladened with appetizers, desserts and wine that greeted the parents when they came to whatever cabin was home base that week to meet the other camp staff and families. While many were traditional moms and dads, it wasn't unusual to have single moms, single dads, grandparents or the sibling of a parent participating with the child. As with any group, some parents were reserved and stood to the side, others wanted to talk to everyone right away, and still others sought out their team of therapists. But when the group divided into teams, (usually five to six teams per week), the small talk ended. Some teams went outside to sit around a picnic table or gather around the firepit, others retreated to the cushy couches in the great room, while another team nestled in the loft.

Once with their team, these families spilled their guts. They talked about their greatest fears and hopes for the week, their greatest challenges, and their greatest joys. They laughed with relief, cried openly, and immediately recognized their common bond. All of them had a special child. A different child. A child who made life overwhelming. A child who brought out all their guilt, anxiety and inadequacy. A child they were unprepared for and may even have felt resentful toward. A child they loved with all their aching heart.

22

Gisela

THE FIRST FULL day of camp always began with parents dropping their special kids off at therapy and bringing the rest of their family to the administration cabin for breakfast. Gisela, who I always referred to as the most important person at camp, prepared a breakfast fit for anyone gearing up for a rigorous hike. Gisela was big on hearty and light on healthy. I did convince her to provide fresh fruit with her biscuits and gravy and famous monkey bread (which was dripping with butter and sugar), but if you were on Weight Watchers, you would probably want to eat before you came. Eggs, bacon, sausage and potatoes usually rounded out the buffet. No one really complained. In fact, there were many dads who considered Gisela's Welcome Breakfast the highlight of the week and would be the first in line every year.

Gisela was hired as our camp cook to prepare the reception for the first night, the welcome breakfast for the families, and dinner for the volunteers and therapists for the rest of the week. We first knew Gisela as the mother of Nina, one of our excellent occupational therapists. But we soon learned that her true identity was that of a robust, tough German survivor of the Holocaust. You did not want to mess with Gisela. Her kitchen was sacred and organized to her liking, so if you were in there, clean up after yourself and leave her stuff alone.

It didn't always make for harmonious relationships with the staff, but their meals were always hot and on time.

The other thing we learned about Gisela is that she loved our kids, our families and was fiercely loyal. She learned the value of family during World War II. Gisela was torn from her family and left on her own when she was only eleven years old. She was raped and abused. She knew hardship and struggle as few do and is an example of strength and perseverance. As no stranger to struggle, she identified with the long way around in life and embraced our families with a depth of understanding and compassion that fueled her deep devotion to Adam's Camp. We were so lucky to have Gisela. We probably wouldn't always have said that when she put the leftovers from the night before into the current night's lasagna or launched into a tirade about an invasion of her kitchen, but Gisela was a perfect example of the grit, dedication and love that defined Adam's Camp. She cooked for us for ten years before her health prevented her from continuing when she was somewhere in her 80s. She probably cooked for five years longer than her health really allowed, but that was Gisela.

After breakfast, the families gathered in the main room of the cabin to learn about the activities available to them the rest of the week. There was always a campfire one night, led by a music therapist, where families gathered to sing and make s'mores. I loved the smell of campfire smoke and burned marshmallows that surrounded our crew while we participated in this favorite camp tradition.

There were also parent support groups available all week. Each morning, the social worker would meet with families interested in discussing behavior, education, working with the system, parent burnout and a hundred other topics related to raising a child with special needs. There was a sign-up sheet available for family photos which were taken by the Snow Mountain Ranch photographer (who, by coincidence, was the photographer who took Bob and my wedding photos).

Before we launched into plans for the rest of the week, I told the story of the founding of Adam's Camp. In order to completely buy in to this unique model of treatment, we thought it was important for families to understand *why* Adam's Camp exists. I am not a big crier. I never have been. But every time I looked into the faces of those moms and dads who have walked the same path we have and saw their eyes well with empathy and knowing, I cried. I cried because I was reliving those early years with Adam and the pain that accompanied them. I cried because I knew the complex emotions these families were experiencing. I cried because it was safe to cry with people who knew. No matter how many times I told the story, I always cried. I still do.

Families left that morning session prepared for the week ahead. All the hopes, fears and plans they had for the week were in full motion. Many families would head out to hike, play mini-golf or swim while others would head straight back to their cabin to rest, read a book or simply sit on the porch and stare at the stunning scenery. Still others would venture into Winter Park or Grand Lake to shop and enjoy lunch at a restaurant. Countless families over the years told us this was the first time they had been alone with their spouse since their child with special needs was born. This was their time to fill their cup and to nurture relationships with the rest of their family. It is hard to measure the value of this respite, but it was not unusual for us to hear that Adam's Camp had saved a marriage.

While we were busy helping children realize their potential and develop their strengths, we were doing the same thing for our families, sometimes without realizing it. We discovered that family time together was as important as our family groups, and in some cases was even more important. We learned to encourage families to take the time their kids were in therapy to feed their depleted souls with whatever they needed.

23

Day One Drama

THAT FIRST MORNING drop-off could be stressful. Many of our campers had spent little time away from their parents and experienced separation anxiety. The team of therapists would welcome the child with the support of the two team volunteers, quickly moving them to an area where there were toys and activities to distract and engage them in the therapy day. Meanwhile, the therapist would quickly learn from the parent how the child had slept and if there were any other circumstances that might affect their day. The kids weren't the only ones with separation anxiety in many cases, and gentle reassurance for the parents was often a part of this transition.

The therapy space was set up the day before in rooms typically used as conference space. They were large, open rooms separated into small, individual therapy spaces by heavy wood dividers. Therapists usually brought a lot of their own materials to add to the growing supply of toys and equipment Adam's Camp provided.

There was a white board posted in every space that outlined each child's schedule for the day. The only times that overlapped for all five of the kids on each team were morning music time, snack, lunch and either therapeutic horseback riding or swim therapy in the afternoon. Otherwise, the kids were experiencing one-on-one therapy and were rotating between the therapists throughout the day.

The first day of therapy was often painful to observe in the early years, especially when there were kids on the autism spectrum on the team. Most of the kids on the autism spectrum, a diagnosis that was starting to become more common in the late 80's, had had no therapy services before attending camp because the diagnosis was so new and many therapists were not trained to work with these kiddos. Many of these kids had no impulse control and some would cry or scream the entire day. The therapist's main goal that first day was to calm them enough to engage them in therapy. Their task was exhausting and seemed to result in little progress. My heart always went out to these dedicated professionals, and in the back of my mind I doubted they would ever return to Adam's Camp after enduring this day of what could only be described as abuse. Many were scratched, bitten or hit and had the scars to prove it.

Eli was one of those early campers. Eli first attended Adam's Camp in 1993 when he was five years old. Eli's mom, Betty, would eventually be divorced from Eli's father which is an all too common occurrence when a child with special needs adds stress to a marriage. Betty would request a cabin as far from other cabins as possible, because Eli would often scream the entire night. Betty had never been away from Eli, nor had she seen any significant progress in his behaviors. The therapy world was just beginning to learn to treat children with severe autism.

The therapy team was prepared to work with Eli. For Betty, the notion of a few hours respite for the week was a God send. This is what Betty says about her years at Adam's Camp:

"At the beginning of each week of camp, parents were asked to list three goals. My goals were always the same. #1- have fun. #2 – have fun. #3 – have fun. Because, back then, we almost never had fun. If Eli could just have some fun, be a kid, and be an Adam's Camper, that would be an important achievement.

"During Therapy Camp years, Adam's Camp therapists created exquisite progress records with photos, including real moments, strengths and abilities, goals, interventions and results, and recommendations. It was remarkable to see photos of Eli having social and recreational experiences I didn't create for him. It gave me hope that someday he might have an independent life.

"Today (25 years and 25 Adam's Camps later) Eli is a model camper. He learned to be a good citizen at camp. He learned to look forward to his own recurring Adam's Camp event. When I drop him off, he turns around and stridently tells me goodbye repeatedly until I leave because camp can't really start until I am gone. And he has his own goals now -#1 – have fun, #2- have fun, #3 – have fun." ~ Betty Lehman, Eli's mom.

For Betty, this time of respite gave her the chance to gather the strength that had been drawn from her after another year of 24-7 care for Eli. Betty was exhausted, and the first thing she did after she dropped Eli at therapy was to head to the local hot springs. She participated in parent programs as well, but for her, the respite was crucial.

Meanwhile, the therapists were able to help Eli and many kids like him transition into this safe and nurturing therapy environment. When I walked into the space the second day of therapy, I was genuinely astounded by the transformation that had already begun with these kids. They were usually much more engaged, already making developmental strides, and the rhythm of the therapy day was becoming far more fluid. Volunteers moved in and out of the spaces, gathering necessary materials, taking photos for reports, and offering other supports as needed. Therapists moved expertly between kids, stopping only to record interventions and results between campers.

Betty would be the first to say the therapy Eli received at camp was critical, but she was a great example of our not knowing exactly what it was about Adam's Camp that was going to be soul changing. What about this experience was going to reach deep enough within her to soothe and feed the soul she was sacrificing to the care of Eli? I know Betty was hoping for a life-changing experience for Eli that would offer her a glimpse of what might be possible for him in the future. I don't know if she was prepared to be reintroduced to herself during the rare break she experienced while Eli was in therapy. You never know when the hot springs will be a catalyst to a soothed soul, but for Betty,

Adam's Camp allowed her the opportunity to soak in the healing waters of Hot Sulphur Springs once a year for over 25 years. And Eli? He proved that the right intervention, support and hope could lead to a model camper who lives a full life, and not only can, but does have enormous fun every year at Adam's Camp.

24

Meanwhile, Back in Recovery...

ADAM'S CAMP MIRRORED my recovery from addiction. The Adam's Camp families were my tribe when it came to raising Adam and living the life of parenting a child with special needs. At Adam's Camp, we leaned into each other. We empathized about the hard stuff and laughed knowingly about the absurd, unique and precious moments that made up our days. I found strength, support and encouragement at Adam's Camp.

My life in recovery was so similar with a whole different tribe and purpose. The other people in AA became my tribe when it came to living a sober life. In recovery, we leaned into each other. We empathized about the hard stuff and laughed knowingly about the absurd, unique and precious moments that made up our days. I found—and continue to find—strength, support and encouragement in recovery.

Community was and is my lifeline. The community of Adam's Camp gave me the resources I needed to give Adam what he needed. The community of recovery saved my life. I know without a doubt I could not have gotten sober without the fellowship.

After we returned to Denver, I found several AA meetings to attend and began to connect to the recovery community in Denver. I continued to work the twelve steps, got a sponsor and reached out to help others. Those were the key ingredients to recovery, and I was on board.

The people in those rooms were all parts of me. I could see them struggle with same things I struggled with. When they were overwhelmed by fear, anxiety or frustration, they all wanted to escape those feelings, and the quickest escape came in a bottle for those of us in AA. I listened in meetings when my fellow alcoholics shared their greatest struggles. Time after time, I watched those with both new and long-term sobriety take their struggles to God, and those who truly leaned into their faith changed. They had found a solution, a "sufficient substitute" as the Big Book of alcoholics anonymous calls it, in their higher power.

Those in the rooms who didn't completely buy into recovery also helped me by demonstrating what happens to people who think they can handle their drinking on their own. Most went out and got drunk. Some died.

I experienced life-giving, trouble-sharing, hope-inspiring sobriety every time I went to a meeting. I was reminded in those meetings of who I was, because on my own, I would have talked myself into the next drink.

I began my life of recovery as a woman who had never lost her home, never got a DUI, was never hospitalized due to drinking, and still had her marriage. I didn't look like someone whose life was in peril. In fact, I didn't believe I was "powerless over alcohol" as the first step of recovery suggests. I knew drinking was a problem for me, but in those early days, I believed I still had some choice about drinking. I had certainly proved I could not stay sober on my own, but at that time in my life, I was simply not yet ready to relinquish all of my pride and control. Control was how I had gotten through my life, so it was hard to imagine turning my will and my life over to the care of God, no matter how great He was. I had a long road ahead.

Still, I loved my sober life. The freedom of not waking up every day either hung over or thinking about when I was going to have the next drink gave me a glimpse of freedom. I was still struggling with eating disorders, so my compulsions were also alive and well, but the hope I had found in sobriety gave me a vision of victory over bulimia as well. As we like to say in recovery, the colors in my life became brighter.

While I thought alcohol enhanced my life experiences, I learned that it actually drained the color out my days. When I drank, all I could see was food and more alcohol. I isolated to keep myself from drinking because, unlike many alcoholics who drink in isolation, my binge drinking took place at parties and events. Even when I was experiencing the feeling of elation when I was drunk, I knew it was an artificial high that would eventually wear off and leave me with regret and a hang-over. It was a vicious cycle. After not drinking for a few days, I would begin to long for that feeling of euphoria that seemed to fill the emptiness I experienced after a few days without booze. Every weekend, the same cycle. I had created a prison I had no idea I was in.

In sobriety, my view went from a myopic, desperate need to control and regulate *everything* to a gradually widening panorama of possibility. At the same time I was recognizing the tight prison walls I had built for myself, I was seeing a glimmer of what lay beyond those walls. I caught a glimpse of an ever-emerging God of the universe and I offered my hand to Him. Well, initially I offered my pinky to Him, but in His graciousness He accepted what I had to offer at the time. He held on just tight enough to let me know He was not going to rule my life before I was ready to let Him. He kept me sober, and that was evidence enough for me to continue to lean into Him and invite Him into the small internal world I had created for myself. I prayed. As I watched my brothers and sisters in AA walk in relationship with their God, I began to understand the difference between believing there is a God and having a personal relationship with Him.

There is nothing more powerful than watching a newcomer walk into AA, defeated, hopeless and often alone, come to life after surrendering to a higher power. I have seen people literally change before my eyes, sometimes quickly and sometimes slowly, time after time. I am working with a woman now whose transformation has been nothing short of miraculous.

Ella (not her real name) came into the program completely broken and hopeless. She was in her mid-40's and had been using drugs and alcohol since she was a teenager. When the use of alcohol and drugs had stripped her and her husband of everything they had, she got sober on her own for a few months, but she was miserable and completely hopeless. It turns out drugs and alcohol were dulling the pain she was in because of an abusive marriage she saw no way out of. She was so diminished by her husband's constant belittling, she had no confidence in her ability to survive as a sober, capable woman.

Ella came into AA because she was at the end of her rope. For a while, she just attended meetings here and there, but eventually she decided she wanted what so many of us seemed to have; peace and serenity in sobriety. She reached out to me to sponsor her and take her through the steps. I had two other sponsees at the time and was not sure I had the time to dedicate to her, but there was something about her desire that led me to believe God had brought us together.

It has only been about two and a half months, but Ella is a completely different woman today. She is working the steps fervently, and most importantly, completely opened her heart to a higher power. In AA, you can choose your concept of a higher power, but Ella calls Him God as I do. She began to pray and listen, went to at least one and sometimes two meetings a day, and looked for ways she could be of service to others. She found and was hired for a job she likes, and her husband is moving out of their house at her request this weekend. She is present for her daughter. While her life is far from perfect, she has found peace. She trusts God will take care of her, and that faith has given her the confidence to reclaim her life.

Being a part of a fellowship where stories like Ella's continue to demonstrate the power of God is a blessing. I know, in my early days in recovery, I clung to the faith of those I knew had found what I wanted. Eventually, I experienced God working in my life in the same way he worked in others. I wish I could say my transformation was as dramatic and immediate as Ella's had been, but it was not. Yet I can say that today, my faith saved my life.

When we first moved back to Denver in 1989, I was what I would call, "Christian Light." I took what made sense to me in the Bible and embraced it while looking past those things that I didn't understand.

I was still not ready to surrender my life and will (aside from alcohol) to a God who would want to change me in any way I didn't *want* to change. I was certain that a life surrendered to the Christian God would likely mean He would want me to go to Africa and be a missionary which I was not down with for a multitude of reasons. I don't like flying long distances, can't imagine evangelizing and am not okay with no running water or electricity. Sorry, but for now it was God *on my* terms.

I had so much to learn about this God I was coming to know better. It never occurred to me my relationship with Him would be one in which His will for me was actually better and far more gratifying than my will for myself.

The journey of recovery is remarkable. Those thirty-plus years ago, I thought my sober life was finally complete, but it was merely the beginning. The small miracles I was experiencing were only a preview of what was to come.

25

Adventure Camp

ONE OF THE most beautiful aspects of our little program was how ready and willing we all were to change and grow Adam's Camp to suit our kids. The therapists working with Adam and other eight year-old campers recognized that while some of our kids still benefited from therapeutic intervention, others were ready for an equally important need which was surfacing more each day—the need to develop appropriate social skills.

In 1992, our "I Can" Camp was born. This camp was designed as a six-day sleep-away camp that included both kids with and without identifiable needs. The goals of the camp were to continue to work on therapeutic objectives while fostering relationships and social skills.

An Occupational Therapist (Greg) and a Speech Therapist (Sharon) developed the program. Adam attended that first year and successfully tried a number of new skills. He hiked, played mini golf, went rafting and even rode the go-carts in Grand Lake with a program volunteer. He helped make pancakes in the morning and cleaned up after himself after all meals.

Attempting all these activities gave Adam a new level of confidence and gave us a new level of expectation. Adam was old enough now to understand that, with the right audience and especially people who didn't know him well, he could play the "I'm disabled" card and get out of doing things he didn't want to do. At Adventure Camp, he was pushed to do things even *he* didn't know he could do. The expectations were high.

So many skills encouraging independence were reinforced and taught at "I Can" Camp. When conflict arose, the counselors took a break in the action to encourage the kids to work it out. When someone tried the zip line for the first time, the other campers were there to cheer them on as peers. At mealtime, everyone had a job and understood their part in the community. Rather than being the kids who were always helped, they became helpers to each other. They rose to the occasion of being separated from their parents, some for the first time ever.

More than anything, these kids had a blast. With the supports provided, they were able to do virtually any activity provided at a typical camp. Their worlds were opened to the many possibilities awaiting them. Rather than viewing themselves as disabled, they started to understand they were just differently abled.

I love Tyler whose story so illuminates the Adam's Camp magic:

"My husband and I are the parents of a 13-year-old boy with a neurological disorder. Our family has been attending Adam's Camp for the past nine years. Each year, our son returns home with new abilities that he/we did not know he had. His speech has progressed so much as well as his physical abilities since he started camp. He went from a shy child to one that will talk your ear off !He used to be afraid to try new things and would quietly watch the other kids. Now, he is ready to try something new, and even if it is scary. Last year, he did the zip line for the first time, and was afraid. This year, he got right on it with no problem, and loved it!

I have been so impressed with the therapists that work with the kids at Adam's Camp. They are there because they want to be there, and they are just as excited about the accomplishments of our son as we are! I also have really enjoyed the parent conferences, which are really informative. Adam's Camp is a wonderful way to meet lots of families who experience the same things that we do day to day. Our experience far exceeds anything we ever expected for our son, and we plan to return every year." Tyler's mom

"I Can" Camp was a jumping-off place for many more experiences that reinforced the sometimes awkward but usually adaptable skills that would mold our kids very special place in this world. The program was a big hit from the get-go. And kids came back enthusiastically each year to enjoy the days filled with everything from the craft shop to archery and evenings backlit by campfires that offered just enough flame to roast the gooey marshmallows that slid easily between the chocolate and graham cracker of their s'mores. Campfire songs and laughter were all that interrupted the starlit stillness of those magical nights. There was the occasional odd wail or unique laugh, and once in a while, a camper would bolt for the woods, but those anomalies melded as naturally into the experience as the breeze fluttering in the aspen.

In the Adam's Camp world, those very unique sounds and events were spice. They were expected, adapted to, and eventually embraced while not always being endorsed. These campers accepted each other with all their quirks and what others would call weirdness.

Not surprisingly, this program grew over the next few years and the campers participating grew as well. As these kids became teenagers, it became clear that Adam's Camp needed to accept a new challenge – helping our campers form lasting friendships with kids like them.

During those years and even today, much emphasis is placed on inclusion. Our kids are being included more and more in regular classes where it is appropriate, and that is positive. But we discovered that, as these campers grew older, their social skills lagged further and further behind those of their typical peers. While they were often treated almost as mascots in school by being elected Prom King or Queen, or being someone's buddy, there were not many typical kids reaching out to them to socialize. Typical teens were busy finding their own place in this world. Our kids needed an opportunity to socialize with kids they could relate to, and those kids were usually others with special needs.

In the summer of 1996 we introduced Teen Camp exclusively for teens with special needs between the ages of 13 and 19. They would enjoy the same activities as the "I Can" Campers with the addition of more responsibility and a talent show and a dance, both of which have remained highlights of the week for this group.

Chairs were placed in rows and the microphone primed for the Tuesday night talent show. Campers belted out the lyrics to the latest Boys to Men or Taylor Swift song at the talent show, whether they could sing or not, and received a rousing ovation. More than one accomplished break dancer took the stage, while groups formed to play kazoos or perform magic. Campers who were usually shy and in the background broke out of their safe places and embraced the enthusiastic response of the audience by performing in some way.

Everyone rocked with abandon at the highlight activity of the week, the dance. The disco ball spun while the boom box blared music as diverse as the ecstatic participants on the dance floor. Everybody was exactly the same at the dance— camper, volunteer and counselor alike. It was as if the campers lack of self-consciousness gave the typical volunteers and counselors permission to dance with abandon as well. Many of these campers had been to school dances, but this dance was different. This dance was their people, and no one paid a bit of attention to how anyone else was dancing unless they were introducing a particularily cool dance move or staring a conga line. This was freedom at its best, and our campers thrived at that dance, surrounded by their true peers.

We learned so much about the value of Adam's Camp to our campers and families from the feedback they gave us in their evaluations.

"My son has attended Adams Camp for five years now. It was not an easy transition to go on his first sleep away camp but

the support and understanding of the staff has made each camp more enjoyable than the one before. This is virtually the only opportunity to sleep away from home without family, surrounded by peers. So important for his independence, self-esteem and socializing." Mom of Teen Camper

"My son has attended Adam's Camp for 25 years. He has learned good citizenship, how to be a friend, how to have fun in social settings as well as enjoying an enormous improvement in his competence and self-esteem. " Adam's Camp Parent

With the goal of developing friendships, we knew that one week a year wasn't going to provide the necessary framework for sustained relationships. We decided we wanted to offer programming through-out the year for these kids, and we began by offering a fall reunion weekend. We have since added unique weekend offerings for campers throughout the year, including a winter dance, road trips, a downtown adventure, and fall getaways to the YMCA sister property in Estes Park.

This camper is a joy to welcome every year and takes advantage of so much Adam's Camp has to offer:

*"Our Son has attended Adam's Camp Adventure Camps, Winter Camps and Annual Dances for over ten years. To say that Adam's Camp is the highlight of his life would be an under-statement. The camps are exceptional, the staff highly trained and welcoming, the counselors motivating and kind. Activities provided by Adam's Camp allow him to develop friendships with other campers and grow as an individual. We would never have imagined that he would experience ziplining, rafting, rock climbing, horseback riding, and tubing. He especially enjoys the dances and Karaoke. Adam's Camp provides respite for the entire family. We are so thankful to have Adam's Camp in our lives "*Parents of an adult camper

It is magnificent to watch our Adventure campers check in for camp. They immediately see their friends and reconnect like long lost relatives if they live far from each other and as familiar friends if they see each other during the year. They generally brim with expectation as they wait patiently with their parents for the health screening and to check in to their cabins.

Not a session goes by that we don't hear messages like these from camper parents, who are so grateful not only for the experience for their kids, but for the respite for themselves.

"Adams camp has changed our family's lives! With our extended family members living out of state we had no one we could leave our son with to have a break from caregivers responsibility. Adams camp has provided that for us. They are our family and I am so appreciative of all the staff and volunteers that care for Nathan. He loves Adams camp and has made so many friends. Would give 10 stars if I could." Nathan's father

The relationships campers built spilled over into the community as we partnered with National Sports Center for the Disabled at Winter Park, where our campers went to ride the Alpine slide and take advantage of the other activities at the resort. The town of Winter Park became our partner when they set out chairs for our campers at their Concert in the Park every Thursday night. The town of Grand Lake rolled out the red carpet for our campers when they arrived on Friday to bowl, ride go-carts, picnic and buy ice cream at one of the shops they browsed through on the main street.

Adam's Camp is filled with all the things you would hope a memory-making week would hold, and our kids remember their adventures all year.

That, it turns out, was the problem the year we were going to have to tell Greg Hauserman he couldn't come to camp anymore because he had turned 19. Every year, when Greg's dad comes to get him after camp and drives him down the hill to his home in Golden, he triumphantly announces: "364 days till Adam's Camp, dad." He announces the number of days *every* day until it is time to return to camp.

I was definitely not the person who was going to tell Greg he could no longer attend, and none of the staff or counselors wanted to be the bearer of that news either. *So*, instead, we created our Young Adult Program. It turns out there is no age limit on fun, and our campers love coming back each year to repeat many of the same activities, because familiar equals comfort for our campers and because it is just plain *fun*. We built new levels of independence into the adult programs, but the basic comradery and soul are the same. Adam's Camp just doesn't get old for many of our campers, and they have all become family by sharing their experience with campers like Greg, whose mom says:

"Greg's experiences at Adam's Camp have most definitely contributed to his sense of responsibility, his social awareness and ability to make new friends, his willingness to follow rules and respect authority, and last, but not least, have given him the gift of looking forward to doing something he absolutely loves once or twice a year"

26

Learn a Little Here, Learn a Little There

THE YEARS ADAM'S Camp spent growing and changing were years of growth for me as well. Being back in Denver and sober were both impetuses for me to re-engage in the mainstream of life, and I jumped in with both feet.

My work with Adam's Camp continued to be rich and exciting. Each season of growth for Adam's Camp brought new challenges, mostly having to do with raising enough money to expand programming and provide scholarships.

In 1991, we received our first grant of $1000 from The Anschutz Family Foundation. It was the first grant I had written, and I will never forget walking into Jeff Pryor's office to present our grant to him. Jeff was the executive director of the foundation, and The Anschutz Family Foundation was one of the few at the time who were willing to take a chance on small organizations in their infancy. This grant opened the door for Adam's Camp to receive funding from other foundations, and our funding base gathered new momentum as we entered the world of grant funding.

When I re-connected with the Junior League of Denver, I chose to work with The Women's Foundation, an organization that championed girls and women's rights and opportunities, as my project. I learned so much from these strong, committed women and was able to help them coordinate events for the organization.

Serving on the Parent Teacher Organization (PTO) and in the classroom at Creekside Elementary kept me up to date with all that was happening at the boys' school. Eventually, I served on the school advisory board and as president of the PTO. As always, all I was learning about fundraising came in handy in this role as one of our primary responsibilities was raising money for the school. More event planning. I was definitely establishing a pattern as I continued to find myself in fundraising roles.

In my years of coordinating events and projects, I have worked with many volunteers. The best of these are incredible, committed people, and many of the Adam's Camp volunteers fall into this category. I think of Jane who was always quick to volunteer for tasks and typically followed through with what she committed to do within 24 hours. She knew her skill set and only took on those things she could do well. Cindy was another volunteer who was a joy to work with. Once she was assigned a task, you knew it would get done. She often went above and beyond by identifying resources and bringing others in to help. Paige was the same way. She was an organizer extraordinaire and once a project or event was put in her hands, she was off and running. Kellie's passion and leadership were both critical to our board for several years. The two Bill's who served on our board were both talented and great resources for the organization.

I have learned so much about working with people through my experience with Adam's Camp, the school, and other organizations. At the end of the day, I believe people want to be heard and they want to be valued. My greatest responsibility as a leader seemed to always boil down to three things. Empower people to utilize their skills by properly training and preparing them for the task, listen to them, and praise them for a job well done. Most any grievance could be resolved if these three things are in place. I tried to rely on these lessons in my work with Adam's Camp.

My work in the community was continuing to equip me as a leader. I know I was way too ego driven in my early roles of leadership, seeking validation like so many stay-at-home moms did in those days. As someone who had relied on position and prestige to bolster my reputation, being home with small kids left me feeling invisible, so when I had a chance to be in charge, I wanted to be noticed for it.

The spiritual growth I was experiencing through my work in AA, bible study and church was helping me to realize that my leadership skills were not something to take pride in. They were a God-given gift, pure and simple. I had been drawn to leadership roles since I was a little girl lording over the sandbox with my insistence on owning the name Mary in our imaginary play. Being at the heart of Adam's Camp and doing the work that allowed us to become sustainable was both fascinating and challenging. When the boys were in middle school, I decided that going to work part-time at an established non-profit would further equip me to serve Adam's Camp. So far, we had been running Adam's Camp off of intuition and what I had learned piecemeal about organization. I wanted to learn more about how established nonprofits operated. I wasn't sure where Adam's Camp was headed, but I did want to know more about how to get there.

Both boys were enjoying school and Bob was continuing to focus on his career, which included a fair amount of travel. I accepted a job as an event coordinator at the Colorado chapter of The American Heart Association. Working with this organization helped me gain a broader view of the non-profit world, make valuable contacts and friends, and receive great training. I was in charge of the Heart Ride, but I decided we should make it into an inclusive event that also offered a walk and roller blading. The name we chose was the Heart Ride, Roll and Stroll, and this event provided a great lesson for me about not trying to do too much.

The event was held on a Sunday at the then-vacated Stapleton Airport in Denver. The walk was held simultaneously at the Rocky Mountain Arsenal, a wildlife center nearby. We all arrived at the venue at 3:00 am to set up for the start of the century bike ride, which started at 7 am. In addition to organizing registration and setting up rest stops on the bike route and walk for the 150 participants; we also had to organize and prepare for the entertainment and food we had secured for the after party. I had a walky-talky that was never silent with questions from the multiple volunteers who were serving. I think the moment I realized I had overreached was when the bagpipe player was sulking by the terminal because his space was taken by the belly dancer who couldn't get her tape to work, so she sat down to eat fish taco's from the vendor who was donating food. The entire day was a madhouse, and I don't think anything went smoothly. We raised a decent amount of money, but surely could have done just as well with a much simpler event.

After four years at American Heart, the Adam's Camp executive director decided to stay home with her kids, and I was ready to take on the role of executive director. My work at AHA had helped me see Adam's Camp was more than ready and able to move into a new phase of development. Fortunately, the board agreed to hire me.

27

The Power To Change

THANKS TO WORKING my program in AA and some outside therapy, I continued to grow emotionally healthier through those years. Demon alcohol was in check thanks to working with a sponsor and being a sponsor to other women like the program instructs. I was able to participate in neighborhood parties (of which there were many) and enjoy the time with friends without using that time as an excuse to get wasted. My bulimia was better, but far from cured during those years. I still had bouts of binging and purging, but they were fewer, shorter, and didn't include as much food as past binges. Since my issues with food began when I was very young, it made sense they were the most difficult to tackle.

I attended some Overeaters Anonymous meetings and the bulk of my work with a therapist was around my eating disorder. My therapist often brought up depression as an underlying condition I may have been treating by binging and purging, but while I acknowledged periods of depression, I was not about to consider medication to treat it. I viewed anti-depressants as synonymous with Valium and other mood enhancers. It took my therapist a few years to convince me I might not be able to deal with my eating issues if I didn't deal with my depression.

I now know depression was a big contributing factor to my

addictions. When I was feeling that sense of sadness and lethargy that defined my depression, I wanted to escape that feeling. I recently wrote a short poem about what that depression, which still visits me every so often, feels like.

Who are you?

You, dropping your cloak of listless sorrow over me, uninvited.

You, who makes my arms and legs heavy, and seeps into my head to block the light.

Didn't you feel me pushing the door shut as you forced your way into my sacred space?

You, so powerful and stifling.

Who sent you? Are you here to dig deeper into my soul, to wrench free the dark caverns shut off to God?

Or are you simply here to steal the joy, the peace ~ the gifts. Why do you surround me with the milky haze that keeps every-one else out? Why do you want me alone?

If you must, teach me. Humble me. Open my soul to new awareness of Him. But if you are here only to destroy me, I will sit with you only long enough to reach Him.

Who are you?

I felt guilty because I had a husband and kids who loved me, a nice home, enough money and dear friends, yet I was not experiencing the joy that reflected my gratitude for all these things. I believed I was being selfish, and I wanted to basically *make* myself feel the appropriate happiness. A drink or a good binge/purge would temporarily lift my spirits. The operative word there is "temporarily".

Once again, I was reluctantly admitting my powerlessness. This time, it was over my depression. I began taking a low dose of Prozac. Within a few months, I noticed a stabilizing of my depression and longer periods of time between binges. Gradually, the binging and purging became less and less frequent. My fear of weight gain was unrealized as I had a healthy exercise routine in place by then, and God knows I had done enough research in my food-obsessed years to understand healthy eating habits. It would be many years before I became binge-free, but my episodes of binging became more sporadic and less intense.

For some people, the recognition of an addiction and its consequences can be enough to catapult them into seeking recovery. They throw themselves into recovery and are able to change difficult, established habits in a relatively short period of time. That would not describe me.

I clung to every addiction until I had absolute proof my life was going to be okay without it. To a non-addicted person, that has to sound crazy. It *actually is* crazy. It took me four years from the first time I walked into an AA meeting to actually stop drinking for more than a few weeks at a time. When I quit smoking, which I had done since I was 18, it was a few years of slowly cutting back between the time I decided to quit and my last cigarette when I was in my late thirties. My eating disorder took literally years to purge from my life (pun intended). For some reason, I am the kind of addict who hangs on until the bitter end. I am grateful God allowed me to recover in spite of my stubborn resistance to change.

In the program of AA, it is said that in order to actually give up alcohol, we have to have a sufficient substitute. In other words, alcohol has served us in a number of ways for a long time. For me, more than anything else, it filled the empty space rooted deep in my soul. I now know that empty space was the one reserved for God, but without

Him, it felt like sadness and anxiety and emptiness. Whatever need alcohol meets within an addict must be met in another way. Our brains are different. My brain latched onto food as the solution when I was a child, then added alcohol and nicotine while I was in college. There were other things I used to fill that hole in my soul as well, but none of them brought the peace I sought.

For an addict, the sufficient substitute had better not be a different substance or another person. It is easy to substitute one addiction for another. Addicts can move from alcohol to drugs or food or sex, continuing to feed escape. The sufficient substitute must be a power greater than the addict. For this addict, and countless others, that power is God.

True to form, I wasn't about to turn my power over to God until I was comfortable that He could fill those needs I was so desperately trying to hide under my addictions. I explored God. I prayed to God. I talked to others about God and listened to countless testimonies about His power in their lives. I went to church and listened to teaching from the Bible with which I had been raised. I participated in a small group Bible study. Ever so slowly, I began to trust God. Over and over again, He showed me that life with Him was enough. As I began to trust Him more and more, He revealed a life with Him that was actually more than enough. I began to experience peace.

As the chains of addiction began to slip from my life, I started to understand what true freedom was. And the best news of all was that it was impossible to abuse my reliance on God. The more I relied on Him, the more peace and freedom I experienced. I surrendered a little more each day to God's power. I continue to surrender more each day, and I am convinced there is no end to the promise of peace and purpose I have gained by seeking this magnificent God. What a gift.

I started each day just asking God to keep me sober that day. I was told to do that by my sponsor, but as I said that prayer each day and the sober days passed, I realized God was doing for me what I could not do for myself. I wasn't fighting as much to stay sober. I felt like I was being *kept* sober.

There is a new playbook when one decides to live a spiritual life. The most important changes I had to make revolved around pride and self-sufficiency. Living on the basis of humility (embracing the woman God created me to be and utilizing the gifts He has given me to live out His purpose) and recognizing that I am not, as I had always assumed, all-powerful over my own life were lessons I learned...you guessed it... slowly.

My need for recognition and to be right began to fade. I started to reflect on my worth through the eyes of God rather than through the eyes of others. My usual m.o. when others would threaten me by disagreeing with me or by acting like they didn't like me was to defend my power and authority by gathering those who did agree with me to bolster my cause and discredit the other person. I did this with a great show of false compassion, mind you, but the truth was, I needed to be right most of the time.

When I began to see myself and others through the eyes of God, my sense of who I am started to shift. Recognizing God's unconditional love for me began to take the pressure off others to make me feel and be okay. Rather than viewing my skills as self-acquired assets, I saw them as gifts I was given. Conversely, I saw clearly that the things I wasn't good at were not failings but were simply not my gifts.

28

Ready...Set...Go.

WHEN I LIVED as an active addict, I had no idea how much time and energy my addictions sucked from my life. I was always a fairly productive person, which allowed me to believe that my lifestyle was a normal one. While spending many a Saturday and/or Sunday nursing a hangover, I still managed to run errands, do things around the house and even plan and execute the next party.

What I didn't recognize was that flurry of activity was me running from the person I was created to be. I believed if I was busy, I was okay. Shopping, pouring over recipes, and cooking fed my eating disorder and my alcoholism while also disguising themselves as the activities of a devoted wife making a good home for her family. I did want to make a good home, but I know that I had other motivations for all things related to food and drinking.

As I surrendered more fully to God and the spiritual life He offered, I pushed further away from food and alcohol as my "go to" solutions to everything. I discovered a reliable connection and eventually an active relationship with God. I became less afraid of my feelings with this new power in my life. I practiced walking through the restlessness, fear and sadness when it came, discovering that resting in those feelings with God could actually bring peace.

The hole in my soul began to heal, and I realized that rather than fill that hole, I could actually let it go. I felt God begin to inhabit every part of me...my mind, my body and my heart. I found that while the comfort provided me by substance never lasted, no matter how much I increased the amount of that substance, the power of God never ran dry. Spirituality was the one thing I tried that was impossible to abuse by seeking more.

Once my mind began to release the constant dance I was in with food and alcohol, I had capacity to think of other people. The selfishness necessary to so rigidly control my life began to dissipate. With God in control, I could share so much more of myself with others. The freedom I felt allowed me to expand the narrow world I had lived in for so many years and begin to make a space for true service. I had always helped others, but usually with a desired outcome for myself. Now, most of my needs were met by my relationship with God. He gave me more than I needed for myself and equipped me to give the rest away.

In my early sobriety, I was still learning the difference between volunteering and service when I was volunteering for The Woman's Foundation. I helped with various clerical tasks but got involved in creating a slide show for one of their fundraising luncheons. The first slide show I created with another woman was impactful and well-received, so I was asked to produce another slide show and to eventually chair their recognition dinner in the spring.

I decided to make the dinner an Italian theme, with photos from Italy, the honorees carrying shopping bags and talking about shopping in Italy, and all speakers saying "Bonjourno", etc. (You get the drift) A member of the Women's Foundation Board had written a song for the honorees which I volunteered to sing as a duet with another woman. The president of the Foundation didn't go for the theme, but I was determined and had already written the script. I was unwilling to change it, so she reluctantly went along.

Looking back, I see how prideful I was. I think the Italian theme was kind of hoaky and detracted from the real point of the dinner which was to honor two amazing women. The song was difficult to sing, and I should have let the other woman sing it solo. I basically sucked and the performance went poorly. I made that dinner all about me. It's embarrassing to me now.

I stumbled greatly on the path to where I am today, and I imagine I will continue to stumble as I work my way closer to the woman God created me to be.

It was with that mindset that I took the reins at Adam's Camp. I wanted to share Adam's Camp with others so their best selves could shine through this work, just as mine had. I had plenty of lessons yet to learn as I continued to check my pride and vanity, but I knew how God was leading me. I know His timing was perfect.

29

Into the Trenches

MY FIRST ADAM'S Camp office as executive director was in downtown Denver in a funky loft space loaned us rent-free by Cactus
Communications, a marketing firm for which one of our board members, Dianna, was a principal. It was a large space with wood floors, a
high ceiling and a loft where we stored the equipment we used for our
Denver-based Early Start Program.

At my side was our program director Jenni Lee. Jenni was a Music
Therapist who introduced the incredible discipline of Music Therapy
to our therapy program. Jenni's love for our special kids fueled her
work at Adam's Camp. Her abundant energy and personality reminded
us all that the work we do and the results we see after a week of intensive therapy are seldom subtle.

Both of us worked part time so were not always in the office at
the same time, but when we were together, we flat out had fun. By
this time, we were nine years into the organization and ready to see
where we could take it. In 1996, we had served 144 clients including
therapy and early start campers and their families and adventure
campers. While we still represented a skeleton staff, we were willing
to do what it took to grow and enhance our programs. We were both
excited by the potential of Adam's Camp, and neither of us were at
a loss for ideas. Jenni and I were both dreamers, and this was the

time for dreaming in the life of the organization. I loved working with Jenni.

While Jenni worked to recruit campers, therapists and volunteers, I continued to manage the fundraising, finances and operations. It seemed we were always in the middle of one fundraiser or another and were working to get the word out about Adam's Camp. Before the internet, our feet and our satisfied families did most of the marketing. We took flyers about our events and programs to toy stores, bookstores, TV stations, pediatrician's offices and anywhere else catering to children.

Jenni continued to reach out to her friends who were therapists, and she built on the corps of pediatric professionals who sustained our therapist base for many years. We hired Tom O'Malley, a young man interested in becoming a speech therapist, to serve as an administrative assistant, and the three of us worked together, helping each other however help was needed. Our motivation was the desire to share the incredible hope and healing we continued to see our families experience through a week at Adam's Camp.

While I had heard countless inspiring stories about campers and their families each year, I was now witnessing, firsthand, these stories being created. I have a special place in my heart for the Hatton family, because of my fond memories of their first session of camp. They checked in with Sam, their son with Down syndrome, and their two older boys. They had driven from Iowa to attend camp, so I was especially hopeful their experience would be a good one.

The other four families on the Hatton team had been together and known each other for several years. They had already established a tight relationship and had the routine of getting together before the initial family gathering that first night. This year's gathering was special because it was camper Ian's birthday. All these families were quick to invite the Hatton's to join them for Ian's hot dog and birthday cake celebration.

I could sense there was a level of hesitancy on the part of Sam's family to join in. I'm sure they felt a bit like intruders in this group of families who knew each other so well. Yet as so often happens at Adam's Camp, Sam represented the bond that quickly folded him and his family into the Adam's Camp family. They tell it best:

"Our 12-year-old son, Sam, who has Down Syndrome, his two older brothers, and we, his parents just spent our fourth summer at Adam's Camp. Initially we attended for the respite for us while our son was in good care. We were amazed and moved by the extremely high expectations, positive exuberance, and the delight in our child by the counselors and therapists. We all left the week feeling like we could all be our best selves all at the same time. We were all so comfortable with the other families in a way we didn't know we needed. We look forward, almost desperately, to reconnecting with each other and families and staff that have become important friends. Snow Mountain Ranch and the Rocky Mountains provide a gorgeous setting. While our sons have not participated officially in the sib's program, a highlight for them is hanging out with other siblings and special needs children. We have received important information and support in a safe setting around topics like puberty, financial planning, and estate planning. For weeks before our return, at the dinner table we ask and answer the question, "What are you most looking forward to at Adam's Camp?" The list is long for all of us. "The Hatton Family

Stories like this one continued to reinforce our belief in the therapy model we created:

"We love Adam's Camp! Our 8-year-old daughter has been attending Adam's Camp every year since she was 2 years old and loves it. She took her first steps learning to walk at Adam's Camp when she was 2 and said her first words at Adam's Camp when she was 4 years old! The therapists here are so amazing,

and our daughter's confidence soars. We have not found an-
other integrative therapy program that surpasses this one. We
have been super impressed with this whole organization and
all that they do for children with disabilities! We will continue
to come here year after year for as long as our daughter needs
it!" Mom of a therapy camper

We wanted to share the same experience this family had had with the countless families of kids with special needs in our community who were isolated, overwhelmed and looking for answers.

Our first goal of providing quality programming was always at the forefront of our work. Adam's Camp was becoming known as the gold standard of treatment in the therapy community. We knew it was important to remain diligent and responsive if we were to maintain this reputation. We listened carefully to our families and therapists and made changes and improvements as we went along.

Jenni carefully monitored the therapy and staff during each camp session. Because each group consisted of five families, we could easily adapt the group to a specific need if it was called for. That constant attention to quality continued to blossom into results like these:

" They are the most incredible professionals that work as a
team to see your child succeed at the same time that' child has
A-blast. We enjoyed it as a family. Atticus made huge strides
that have stuck at home. I hope they let us come back every
year - they're incredible people." Parent of a Therapy Camper

We were always on the lookout for ways to promote Adam's Camp. We were often asked to speak at the meetings of local service organizations such as the Rotary or Lion's Club. More than once, that organization would in turn raise money for us through an event the organization implemented. We also spoke at schools, professional organizations and other non-profits as well as parent groups. Whenever we were asked, we found a way to share the good news of Adam's Camp. More than once, I attended 7 am breakfasts to sing the praises of Adam's Camp to a Sertoma, Rotary or Kiwanis group

In the early days, before the population explosion in Denver, we could count on media appearances on both radio and television prior to our annual children's concert. Adam and I took early-morning or late-afternoon drives downtown to appear on the news stations to promote our annual event and to talk about Adam's Camp. Adam and I both were comfortable in front of the camera, though Adam was definitely unpredictable! His funny comments were often the highlight of the broadcast. Our events were covered by media as well. The 1980s and 1990s were the glory days for Adam's Camp when it came to media coverage.

As hard as we worked to get the word out, our very best sources of new clients or donors were always our families and therapists. Hearing what Adam's Camp had done for families from those who had been there brought many more families into the fold as we began to experience substantial growth after 1997.

One of the greatest deterrents to people applying to camp was the cost. Because our camp is a therapy program offering 30 hours of one-on-one therapy to each child over five days, Adam's Camp is expensive to run. The actual value of the experience to a family is far greater than what we charge because we subsidize over fifty percent of each camper's tuition through fundraising, but to a family living paycheck to paycheck, it can still be out of reach. Many times, the families who have the fewest resources need Adam's Camp the most. The financial stress added by raising a child with special needs drives many families into crisis. Any extra income they have is devoted to therapy and medical care for their child.

Hearing these families fight for their children and describe the lengths to which they have gone to acquire services for them is both heartbreaking and inspiring. Rarely did I hang up the phone after talking with a dedicated parent without already beginning to figure out a way to help them come to Adam's Camp. These families where a parent may have lost their job, been recently divorced, or be barely existing paycheck to paycheck, desperately needed hope, respite and renewal.

We knew early on we wanted to make Adam's Camp available to our most financially stressed families.

We created a scholarship fund to which any family could apply. Much of our fundraising was devoted to funding scholarships. We offered donors the opportunity to fund an individual family. After camp, we would send the donor a thank-you with photos of the camper and a brief description of their progress at camp. These families often wrote their own thank-you notes to the donor. Personalizing donor's gifts made their support more meaningful to them, and this became a popular way for people to give.

Between helping families identify other sources of funding, facilitating submission of insurance for the families who had insurance for therapy, offering payment plans and giving scholarships to the most challenged families, we have rarely, if ever, turned a family away for financial reasons.

Gradually, I learned that leadership is not about *doing* as much as it is about empowering *others to do*. Everyone has a skill, and a good leader can identify that skill and position a volunteer or employee to make the project or organization better by utilizing their skills well.

When Kim came to work for us as my assistant, she was clearly highly organized and capable. While she was charged with much of the clerical work involved in getting camp up and running, I could see she was capable of higher-level tasks. Eventually, she was involved in grant writing and overseeing event management. She was not one to be in the limelight, but she was an incredibly detail-oriented partner. We were a perfect complement to each other with her great attention to detail and my big-picture thinking and love for spreading the word in front of groups.

Another skill I learned, sometimes the hard way, was how to help people work more effectively together. I found the best way to build a team was to continually focus on the strengths of the members of that team, to quickly admit when I had made a mistake, and to make it ok to fail. At the same time, I tried to set high expectations for communication and commitment. I knew it was my responsibility to set the tone for the culture, and I took that charge seriously while not taking *myself* too seriously. In all things, we had to laugh.

Still, my pride was challenged at every turn as people continued to praise me for my wonderful accomplishment in starting Adam's Camp. But when I was brought to my knees by alcoholism, I made a decision to turn my will and life over to the care of God. I saw I could do nothing of lasting value on my own when God granted me sobriety, and I am clear to this day there is no way I could have started and sustained Adam's Camp without the support and belief of the hundreds of people who saw our mission and wanted to help.

I had many moments that tested my humility and growth. One such moment came when I was working with a very capable, dedicated volunteer who was chairing Adam's Camp's major family fundraiser. Ellie (not her real name) called me the night before the event which would represent the culmination of many months of work and planning. I was expecting a question about some detail regarding the fundraiser, but instead was met with an angry barrage of accusations about my lack of support of her and how I had taken advantage of her over the course of past several months.

I was stunned, confused and hurt. I truly was blindsided. I had no idea she was unhappy and frantically searched my mind for what I had done to bring on this reaction. I apologized for making her feel this way and assured her I would do my best to support her the following day.

In the past, I would have called several committee members to tell them what had happened and would have sought reassurance about the invalidity of Ellie's claims in order to protect myself and make myself appear blameless. Instead, I only talked to one other trusted friend to get her take on the type of support we had offered and to talk about what we could have done better.

While I was definitely rattled by this confrontation, I made the decision to seek to understand rather than to be understood. Ordinarily, my pride would have caused me to defend myself and deflect the blame on Ellie. Instead, I asked for counsel, looked for ways my communication was incomplete and misleading in the distribution of tasks, and finally made an effort to see the situation from Ellie's perspective.

Believe me, that response was not automatic. I wanted to defend myself and arm myself with righteous indignation. Yet I was learning that living life on a spiritual basis is a choice, not a divine intervention that automatically renders my heart and motives pure.

While Ellie did step away from Adam's Camp after the event, I have seen her in different settings since this event. She is cordial and I once again see the good heart she has. Because I chose to respond differently than my pride would have me in a difficult situation, I preserved a relationship and prevented a resentment. Most importantly, I came one step closer to God and one step further from my pride.

I can see in retrospect my spiritual growth was dovetailing with the growth of Adam's Camp while I worked as executive director. Adam's Camp was at a jumping-off place, and I was ready to lead us into the next chapter of our life as an organization. Before my life of sobriety opened the pathway to God, I believe I had the leadership skills to continue our programs and services. What became different for me was my motivation. I was able to see more clearly that this work was God's plan all along and I needed to credit Him for its success and growth while recognizing the people he placed in our path were just His well-meaning children, doing the best they could.

30

The Day Is in the Details

WITH THE EXCEPTION of the two Early Start programs we held in Denver, we spent the entire year preparing for our summer programs held at Snow Mountain Ranch. I suspect God chose me to create this "intensive therapy" concept because I am a big-picture person who is not easily intimidated by the details. That is *not* always a strength, by the way. The real reason I am not intimidated by the details is that I don't have great vision for the details. While others are calculating the numerous tasks associated with implementing this program, in my mind, I am all the way to the outcomes.

Another area I had little respect for were the risks involved in working with kids with special needs in an outdoor environment. Can you imagine the number of things that could go wrong? What if these fragile children were injured trying new activities designed primarily for able-bodied kids? What if they had an allergic reaction to a bug bite or fell off the zip line? How did we really know if the people we hired to work with these kids were reliable? What if these fragile children were accidentally fed something that caused a severe reaction? How could we possibly meet the needs of kids who were non-verbal? The risks were endless. I suspect that was a big reason no one had tried this method before. In my mind, these were challenges that could be overcome and were far outweighed by the potential benefits

In addition to the risk, I don't think anyone in their right mind would ever have created a program that cost so much, involved so many interrelated logistics, relied on as many volunteers and involved as great a commitment from staff as Adam's Camp did. That was just blind faith, which at the time, many of us had.

By the time I experienced my first summer of camp as executive director, we were in our ninth year. While many of our processes were in place, there was still much to be done before we became a well-oiled machine. Actually working in the trenches gave me a complete picture of what we had taken on.

In the summer of 1997, Jenni, Tom and I went up a day early to gather the equipment from the storage shed we rented in Tabernash, a very small town just outside of Snow Mountain Ranch. This involved a U-Haul and a lot of schlepping of equipment and supplies, but the biggest and arguably most important commodity was the food.

Not only did we have to supply snacks for the teams for the week, we had to bring the enough food to feed the staff, volunteers and the Adventure Campers as well. Eventually we were able to contract with the same food supplier used by Snow Mountain Ranch to deliver food to us at the beginning and middle of the week, but in the early days, we schlepped everything there. Gisela the cook was a miracle worker. Snow Mountain Ranch gave us some space in the walk-in refrigerator, but she stored everything else in one refrigerator in our home base cabin. We all ate well, and I usually left at the end of the week with a bag of Gisela's meatballs which I crave to this day.

There were many late nights for the program directors and a few volunteers the day before the staff and campers arrived as they organized what each team needed for the week.

The following day, when staff and volunteers arrived, I reflected on all it had taken to get them there. The actual identification of qualified staff and volunteers was the hardest part, but not the most tedious. After they were hired, this contract staff had to fill out paperwork, provide proof of licensure (for the therapists), attend training and become familiar with their campers by reviewing the forms filled out by the families. Jenni honed her cat-herding skills by spending hours on the phone following up and making sure the staff had completed and mailed forms. In the world without the internet, employment forms were mailed back and forth as was family background information. The copy machine was in constant motion during the months before camp.

Families arrived late in the afternoon on that first day, and visions of all the paperwork and planning that went into getting *them* there filled my head as well. From the moment they applied for camp months before, the process of collecting background information, placing the kids on the right team, accommodating for their particular needs, assessing the need for sibling support, and assigning lodging began.

When the first day of actual camp rolled around, the hours and intricacy of scheduling with our partners came into full focus. Our therapy teams had to be slotted into canoeing, swimming, therapeutic horseback riding and rock climbing at Snow Mountain Ranch.

Adventure Campers were scheduled for swimming, zip line, archery, canoeing, the campfire ring and arts and crafts. Rooms were reserved for the big dance. With National Sports Center for the Disabled, our Adventure Campers were scheduled for an activity day at the Winter Park Resort as well as rafting on the Colorado River on a different day. In Grand Lake, we planned times for bowling, go carts, a picnic in the park and shopping for the last day of the week. All this planning was for multiple teams of campers which has grown to 250 campers over the course of five weeks each summer.

Meanwhile, the siblings were participating in their own program that included some of these same activities. Parent meetings had to be planned. I have vivid memories of Jenni and Tom driving from group to group, attending to the latest "crisis", some of which were a result of lack of good planning or just the need for another gallon of milk, but most of which were just the expected unexpected.

It was at the end of that first day of camp that I marveled every single year. I just couldn't believe we had actually pulled it off…again. The magnitude of the task seemed undoable and ridiculously complex.

Snow Mountain Ranch was overrun by around 100 Therapy campers and family members as well as an additional 50 Adventure campers, moving from one activity to another, each one relying on us to provide them exactly what they needed at that moment. And for that moment, what seemed ridiculously complicated became perfectly possible.

31

The Year of the Ironman

I LOOK BACK with such gratitude on those days, not only because of the joy I experienced in my work, but because I was present to appreciate it. I know, had I still been drinking, the color of that time would have been dulled and compromised. For me, the partying, the hangovers and the remorse I felt in that cyclical life I had created consumed way too much of me. In retrospect, I can now see the energy I poured into my addiction was energy sapped from the life I was created to live.

1997 was the year of The Ironman. Bob finally made his way into this grueling championship triathlon, a goal he had set for himself several years before. In case you don't know what this race entails, it is a 2.4-mile swim followed by a 112-mile bike ride followed by a 26.6-mile marathon. All. At. Once. The training required to complete this event was, as you can imagine, intense. Bob took a sabbatical from work to train, and his heart, soul and mind were consumed. My energy in that season was needed to fulfill my mom duties in addition to my work.

The boys were teenagers in high school. Adam received great services at our neighborhood high school, Eaglecrest, and was blessed with a team of wonderful teachers. He was mainstreamed into some classes that suited him and participated in a contained classroom where appropriate. I still think his class went to Taco Bell one too many times to practice eating out and using money, but nothing is perfect.

The only real troubling incident Adam had in High School was the day he told a fellow classmate her boobs looked like cantaloupes. Sexual harassment was (as it should have been) frowned upon, so Adam was expelled for a day. In the school's defense, he became much more cautious about those types of comments.

Adam's health remained stable during these years although he had developed a seizure disorder which was not unusual for people with cerebral palsy when they went through puberty. His seizures were focal in nature which means they were not grand mal, the severe types of seizures that cause loss of motor control. Instead, his eyes would dart, his heartrate accelerate, and if the seizure progressed, his lips would smack. He was medicated for the seizures, but if he had breakthrough seizures, the antidote was another medication. He experienced seizures about once a month. By this stage of his life, he was pretty much through the hamstring lengthening, heel cord release, and other orthopedic surgeries he would endure to maximize his function.

Adam continued to love police officers and focused on meeting as many officers as he possibly could. He and the school security guard were best buds. The friends he had in the police department were kind to Adam, and he had lunch or rides with them on a regular basis. For Adam's tenth birthday party, one of his police pals came to the house in his squad car and took all the boys for a ride. He once rode in the police helicopter with the Denver Chief of Police. I don't even remember how that came about.

Adam was a part of the Arapahoe County Sheriff Department Explorer Program and took part in weekly meetings where young men and women over 16 learned about life as a police officer. It was during this time he came to terms with the fact he would never be physically or cognitively able to be a police officer. He accepted that reality the same way he accepted all things. He sought out the opportunities available to him and forged ahead with gusto. As he got older, this included scheduling police ride-alongs for himself. Our vacations always included a tour of a police station accompanied by a ride-along for Adam.

While he continued to be funny and great to be around most of the time, Adam still struggled with impulse control and was inappropriate enough to spend quite a bit of time in his room during his elementary and middle school years. These episodes were never violent but were generally verbal attacks on one member of the family or another. I don't remember any specific instances other than the one where he flipped me off on his way to his room. It got to the point where he didn't even have to be told to go to his room. He just went. He took some time to regroup, then reappeared and apologized. It was a process for him that took longer than it does for many of us due to his brain injury, but he made progress just the same.

Jared was at Regis Jesuit High School, an all-boys school where he made good friends who are still some of his best friends today. Academically, Jared excelled at the things he loved and struggled with the things he didn't. He continued to be a good writer and had a love for art, but math and science were challenging. He was an average student, and our hardest times were report card days. But Jared saw no reason to commit to things he didn't like and was not particularly motivated by getting into a particular college.

He liked poetry and loved participating in Open Mic Nights at the local coffee shop. He also worked from the time he was 16 to earn extra money, and he preferred working to extra-curricular activities at school. He had a few girlfriends and enjoyed time with his small group of friends who were as eclectic as he was.

Jared was a fun guy to be around and mirrored his dad's humor to a tee. He describes his humor as absurdist. Bob and Jared engage in long conversations about B movies, tongue-in-cheek you tube videos, and well-done parodies of the current social climate. They also picked up the tradition of playing chess together Bob had shared with his dad. They can entertain each other for hours.

When Jared was very young, he started biting his fingernails. That's not that uncommon for kids, but I mentally stored that information, along with the knowledge that he was inclined to avoid conflict. We didn't notice him drinking in high school, and I had conversations with him about his grandfather and me setting him up for a genetic predisposition to alcoholism. There were, however, a few instances when I was sure I smelled cigarette smoke on him. His explanations for this were always pretty unbelievable. Once, he told me someone had handed him a cigarette to hold for them, but it wasn't just a regular cigarette, but a huge, oversized one. He wasn't a great liar. I worried about substance abuse with him, as any good alcoholic would, but his high school days seemed relatively substance-free.

Because of his rigorous academic schedule, Jared was unable to go with us to Kona, Hawaii, to share the Ironman experience with Bob, but Adam and I went and celebrated with him as he crossed the finish line after 13 hours and 28 minutes. What a feat. Again, I was so happy to be truly present in all ways with him to relish this accomplishment. Since he finished well after dark, my drinking self would have had to celebrate with a few beers before I saw him, which would not have been well received.

When Bob went back to work after his sabbatical, changes were taking place at his company and he was let go. While it wasn't long before he found another job with one of the clients he had worked with, I was once again present to support him during this time. My sobriety was a gift to all of us, especially during that year.

It is impossible for me to imagine all the ways our lives would have been different had I still been drinking, but I have no doubt my 16-year-old sons would have noticed how I handled stress. I know that my husband would have had my drinking as an added stress in his life while he experienced his professional transition. I know my work life would have suffered and I most certainly would have been drinking at Adam's Camp which is not an example I would have wanted to set for others. I would not have been available in the way I was for our boys when Bob was so consumed by the Ironman.

I was certainly still on a path to recovery. My eating disorder was better, but still active as I was experiencing episodes of binging and purging every few weeks. Yet I had a glimpse of life with God, a support system through the fellowship of AA, and a magnificent purpose to which I grew more devoted as the wonder of hope and healing revealed itself in new ways all the time at Adam's Camp. The people who became my friends through AA and Adam's Camp reflected this new way of life as I fell into a rhythm of peace and contentment.

I wasn't yet the woman God had created me to be, but I was much healthier emotionally, physically and spiritually than the woman I had been.

32

Growing Pains

THE FOLLOWING YEARS directing Adam's Camp were filled with learning, meaning and so many stories. It was as if I had a clear outline of what Adam's Camp was and could become, and now was participating in coloring in the canvas.

My organizational skills were most certainly put to the test as we continued to seek the most efficient, effective ways to run our programs. Processes came and went as we continued to improve not only what we did, but how we did it.

One of my least favorite parts of the job was moving. And move we did. Relying on the generosity of others inevitably resulted in frequent uprooting. Over the next four years of enjoying reduced rents from friends, we moved our office three times when those spaces were needed by the owners. After spending five years in an office we outgrew, we spent over ten years in the office from which I retired.

It was during the years between 2001 and 2006 that our growth supported additional staff. As with our programs, that growth was determined by our administrative and program needs Jenni had young children and her Music Therapy practice so had moved on as program director.

As so often happened at Adam's Camp, a friend and board member I had become close with through fundraising work with Partners in

Pediatrics was at the perfect time in her life to come on board as the new program director. She had executive director experience at another non-profit and was passionate about the work of Adam's Camp. The position evolved from part-time to full-time. We then hired full-time office manager to oversee the administrative functions of both program and the office. Finally, we added a part-time position for an adventure camp coordinator.

By this time, we were serving over 400 clients a year through 26 sessions of camp which included mountain therapy, adventure camp and early start. There was no longer a "down time" of year as we were busy planning for the following summer, a spring or fall early start or an adventure camp retreat all year. Additionally, the task of fundraising grew in proportion to the number of clients we served. Our goal remained providing a 50% subsidy for each camper in addition to scholarships for the most financially challenged.

Fortunately, between insurance, program service revenue paid by the families, funding from the particular agency serving the family through their county, fundraising events, grants and fundraisers others held in support of Adam's Camp, we were able to make budget every year with a little to spare.

As executive director, I was in charge of finances. I took care of billing, banking and payroll. I was the brunt of many jokes in this capacity as it was well known that I am not a great "detail" person. We were fortunate to have one of the founders of FirstBank, the second largest bank in Colorado, on our board of directors for several years. He was as kind and fun loving as he was savvy. I still share the story of the look on his face when he asked me if the bank account had balanced, and my response was, "Almost." Close counted in my book, and as I said, we were financially healthy.

One of my favorite hiring stories centers around our need for someone to work a few hours a week to bill insurance for our therapy camp clients. One day, I was engaging in some retail therapy at one of my favorite discount clothing stores when I ran into Laura Johnson, our first executive director. Laura had left the job as ED when her third child was born. I was filled with so many wonderful memories of her time with us, and when I asked her what she was doing, she mentioned she was thinking about getting a part-time job. Laura was notoriously good with the details and was familiar with insurance billing, so I asked her on the spot to consider coming back to Adam's Camp to bill insurance for us.

Laura started a few weeks later with the intention of working about five hours a week. We all loved having her there, and it wasn't long before I realized Laura was a perfect person to take over the position of Finance Manager. After just a few months, I presented this brilliant idea to her and was met with her infections laugh. But after thinking about it awhile, she took on that role and remained in that position for over 10 years.

Laura became my confidante in an office of people of all ages, aptitudes and temperaments. We were like-minded in our values centered around a strong work ethic, an intolerance for drama and a client-first workplace. I loved our staff, but there were always challenges in an office of different personalities, and I was grateful to have Laura to help me navigate some difficult situations.

To be honest, I was also happy to have Laura to roll eyes with. You know what that's like. When you are around people who want to make their problems your problems, or who may have an inflated view of what the big things are, sometimes an eye roll with someone who understands is all that is necessary to neutralize the situation for you. It didn't happen often, but when an eye roll was needed, Laura was my girl.

I really believe Adam's Camp was a labor of love for everyone who worked there. What I am most proud of is the culture we were able to build as an organization. The values of open communication, honesty, service and integrity were constantly reinforced within the office and throughout the summer contract staff and volunteers. Adam's Camp is a group effort. Every link must function from the heart of these values if we are to be successful. We instruct contract staff to check their ego at the door when they work with a team.

Our kids matter most, and for us to serve our kids well, our personal agendas must come second.

In order to hold these values well, I knew every person who worked for Adam's Camp needed to feel valued and heard. I made it a priority to let everyone know how much their role mattered to our work, and to listen to their input regarding that role. I was quick to admit my mistakes and encouraged others to do the same, knowing we learn and grow through those mistakes. Finally, it was an absolute requirement to laugh. We always had great fun, knowing that we could take our work very seriously without taking ourselves too seriously.

I was certainly not perfect at implementing this culture. One of the most challenging and difficult learning experiences I had was at the expense of my dear friend who was serving in the position of program director. Over time and after several years of last-minute hires and hastily formed therapy teams, I could see that my friend was not the right person for that job. She had some wonderful skills, but detailed organization wasn't one of them.

While I had talked to her about the need to tighten up the logistics for camp, I had not informed her in advance that I was thinking of letting her go. It was painful as I truly loved her and did not want to be in this position. I agonized over this decision for months and consulted some of my board members who had been in management about the best way to make this break. I was advised to be quick and decisive when I talked with her, giving her the reasons for the dismissal.

When I finally found the courage to have the conversation with my friend, she was shocked and incredibly hurt. My dismissal of her came out of left field as far as she was concerned as I had never given her any direct warning despite my months of considering this move. She had no idea the situation was that serious.

In retrospect, I can see that, while she had goals to improve her performance, there had never been any consequences attached to not reaching those goals. I didn't want to say the words: "If you don't reach these goals, it may be time for you to consider a different job." Also, I knew the advice I had been given about how to terminate her was not appropriate for someone who was not just an employee but was also a dear friend. I didn't trust my gut, and that was another mistake I made.

I am so grateful I was in recovery during this time, which gave me the tools to look for my part in my friend's anger and hurt. But even though I made amends to her, I lost that woman as my friend over her termination. To this day, it is my greatest regret as executive director. I learned two valuable lessons. One, there should be no surprises when it comes to an employee's performance. Staff should routinely be kept up to date on areas in which they need to improve, areas in which they are doing well and the consequences for not reaching mutually agreed upon goals. Second, I must defer to my instincts when it comes to talking to employees with compassion and love. It may not always work out, but my part will feel clean and I will remain in my integrity.

I was grateful for my recovery and I was grateful for Laura during that time. She encouraged and supported me when I was doubting myself. A close confidant is critical in any leadership role, and Laura was that to me. Laura and I remain very close friends today.

33

...And More Growing Pains

MY LIFE WAS full in the late 1990s and early 2000s. The work I was doing for Adam's Camp had come full circle as I embraced the challenge of directing the organization. I was nurturing my spiritual life as we had re-engaged with church and I participated in a small group bible study I had joined shortly after we returned to Denver. Regular exercise was a part of my life; I had developed a love for cycling that fueled my motivation.

My eating disorder was still present during those years as I was still purging when I overate. The actual binging was all but gone, but I still obsessed about my weight and hated feeling full. Binging no longer held the power of relief it use to as I saw these episodes become infrequent. I felt confident about recovery from my addictions and used my bible study as the touchstone for any personal issues in my life. After all, I had come to believe that God was the answer to all my problems. I went to very few AA meetings because I believed my recovery hinged on my relationship with God, and I was nurturing that relationship through my bible study and church. I had lost contact with most of the people in those rooms with whom I had shared my recovery from alcoholism.

In the spring of 2002, Bob and I went to Florence, Italy, to meet up with Jared who was completing a semester abroad through a program at the University of Colorado where he attended college. We landed in Munich, Germany, rented a car and made our way south through stunning countrysides and mountain passes. We stayed in small bed and breakfasts and were enchanted by the little bakeries that filled their small-towns with the aroma of fresh-baked everything. Our travels took us through Austria, and though it wasn't our first time there, we were once again awestruck by the picturesque chalets, each featuring window boxes overflowing with brilliant flowers framed by vivid green hillsides.

The journey from Munich to Florence had been beautiful and serene. Bob and I were both excited to meet up with Jared the day after we arrived. I clearly remember being seated for dinner after checking into our room at the small hotel. I don't remember being especially anxious, stressed or tired, although it is possible I was feeling any one of those things to some degree as a result of travelling. The waitress came to take our order, and after 13 years of sobriety, I ordered a glass of wine. Somewhere in the back of my mind, that drink was waiting patiently. It was waiting for me to be separated from my world of recovery, and what better place to rear its ugly head than in another country?

God bless my dear husband. Although I'm sure he was both shocked and alarmed, all he said was: "What do you think the people in AA would say about this?" My response? "I don't really know anyone in AA anymore, so I doubt anyone would care." I drank the glass of wine, savoring every sip and paying attention to what it felt like. I felt the buzz, the warm feeling as it slipped down my throat. After dinner, we went back to our room.

The next day, we met Jared and that night had dinner with his host family. They were lovely people with whom Jared had clearly made a strong connection. They served champagne, and again I indulged. I think I had two glasses. I would have loved to have had more, but I knew that would not have been well received by Bob.

The following day, we travelled to Cinque Terre and hiked the hill towns. Again, that night I had a glass of wine. Again, more would have been better.

I know the alluring warmth of the wine I drank in Italy was drawing me back to drinking, but I don't remember being alarmed or concerned. It wasn't that I denied my alcoholism as so many do. I knew I was an alcoholic. I just didn't care at the time. I think I figured this time I could manage it. I didn't project about what would happen when I got home or consider whether I would continue drinking. It's possible I thought I only drank wine because I was in a foreign country and that didn't really "count." I honestly can't remember

When I got home, I called a good friend I had actually attracted into recovery. I was telling her about our trip, and casually mentioned I had enjoyed a glass of wine or two. Her response was jarring to me. She completely flipped out and was clearly surprised and shocked by this revelation.

"You WHAT? Karel! What in the world were you thinking?"

It wasn't until that moment that I realized what was at stake and how dangerous it was for me to drink. It was as if I was startled sober. I knew she was right.

The next day, I went to an AA meeting, I attended meetings for about a month before I acknowledged to the group I had relapsed. I had been sober for 13 years at that point, and I now had to start over. I wouldn't say I was humiliated as I know people relapse all the time, but I was not happy that I would have to start my journey over at day one. It seemed a long way back to 13 years.

Not long after admitting my relapse, I asked a woman I respected to sponsor me. I knew I would have to go through the steps again to discover what it was that lead me to that drink after so many years. Judy was the right person to guide me to that awareness.

I would like to say the next several months were easy and by jumping right back into the program, my life became happy, joyous and free. They weren't easy. They were some of the most difficult and painful of my life. What I found was that I was, as we say in the rooms of AA, spiritually unfit. I was restless, irritable and discontent. I had become disconnected with my alcoholism by leaving the program of recovery, and I lost sight of who I was. I was and am an alcoholic. Alcoholism is a mental, physical and spiritual disease I thought I had tamed. But while I now was not drinking, the "isms" had returned with a vengeance. The peace I had worked so hard to gain became illusive, even though I was enjoying my work. From the outside, my life looked great. On the inside, I was struggling.

My sponsor patiently worked me through this relapse with love and truth. I came to believe, once and for all, that my disease wanted to own me. If I were to remain sober and have a relationship with the God I had come to so strongly desire, I would have to treat my alcoholism for the rest of my life. Again, I surrendered. But this time, I accepted the knowing that God would keep me sober only as long as I continued to seek him not only through my faith, but through the lens of who I am. I can only see that clearly in the rooms of AA because I am an alcoholic.

God remained faithful throughout that year. I began to heal, and the challenges I had been running from I finally faced head on. I gained a deeper understanding of how much I sought validation through others. As I worked the 12 steps, I began to trust God more deeply and completely. I saw that He was doing for me what I could not do for myself.

I would never want to repeat that time in my life as I painfully came to deeper terms with my prideful need to be seen through some very personal experiences. But I believe God's timing is perfect. I know my walk with God would be languishing at the bank of the river of commitment I wouldn't cross had I not gone through this experience. Some people need to be knocked alongside the head with a two by four every so often. I seem to be one of those people.

Today, I have 18 years of this new sobriety. It is a completely different sobriety than I had the first 13 years because it is now wholly a part of who I am, and I am filled with gratitude. I know the sobriety and faith I have today informs every corner of the woman God created me to be. I live a life of freedom, acceptance and much joy thanks to the great love of God I experience every day. Life is still life, and I continue to have my ups and downs. But at the heart of it all is a peace that passes understanding, as the bible says. My reconnection to AA, which had brought me back to God in the first place, continues to heal a broken part of my life that is only understood and transformed in the company of those who share this disease, and more significantly, this solution.

I may not know what is next, but I am grateful and committed to the One who does.

34

More Than His Share

AS IT TURNS out, my most difficult year at work was a very difficult year at home as well. This time, it was regarding Adam.

Sometime in the fall of 2007, when he was 27 years old, Adam began to complain about a pain in his side. We went through the normal sequence of waiting it out, taking antacids, trying to determine if it was a muscle problem and so on. Finally, he declared the pain severe enough to warrant a visit to the ER.

Adam has a high tolerance for pain. He had been through enough splitting headaches and surgeries to understand pain, and he rarely overstated his condition. So, we went to the ER. He had a CAT scan and was diagnosed with a hematoma in his abdomen. The staff asked if Adam had fallen recently, and neither Adam nor we could remember a recent fall that could have resulted in such an injury.

Adam was given pain medication to wait out the healing. He took the medication, but the pain persisted. Again, about a week later, we went to the ER and the test once again indicated a hematoma. His pain medication was increased, and we were sent home.

We kept a close eye on Adam, and he actually seemed to feel better for a time. But a week and a half later we returned to the ER with Adam in unbearable pain. He cried out on the exam table, in an agony we had never seen him experience through all his surgeries or headaches. I remember my own tears of agony, knowing that something was not adding up but feeling powerless to help. We were at the mercy of the doctors, and again the only solution seemed to be to go home, this time equipped with more than one fentanyl patch for pain.

Early on a Saturday morning a few days later, we were back in the ER, and yet another CAT scan was performed. This time, a different doctor came to us with entirely different news. Adam did not have a hematoma. He had a tumor.

We were stunned. Adam had been suffering for a month with a misdiagnosis. The staff decided to air lift Adam to Aurora Medical Center in what we now believe was overcompensation for a long and painful mistake on their part. We drove to the hospital to meet him and arrived about 10 minutes before the helicopter. An ambulance would have been a better option.

Adam was admitted and hooked up to an IV with yet more pain medication. He remained in the hospital over the weekend and on Monday had a biopsy. By that time, we were not surprised to hear that Adam had testicular cancer. What *was* difficult to hear was the oncologist's assessment of Adam's condition. His tumor was too large to remove. It had grown close to his spine and had tendrils that had invaded many delicate areas around it. The tumor would need to be reduced in size before they could remove it. He would need to have chemo before surgery could even be considered.

The next week, Adam started chemotherapy. He tolerated the treatment incredibly well. I imagine it was no worse (and probably not as bad) as the incredible pain he had been enduring as the tumor continued to grow. His oncologist told him he was a much better patient than most of the young men he treated. This was not Adam's first rodeo with surgery and pain, and he took the discomfort in stride as he had done so many times before.

Bob and I took turns taking him for treatments at the oncologist's office where he flirted with the nurses and became a favorite immediately. The outpouring of support from friends and family members was a tender reminder to us of how much Adam was loved. Many people brought meals, gifts, cards and flowers. My brother shaved his head in support of Adam.

I think others, like us, were stunned that Adam had cancer. Hadn't Adam had his allotment of life challenges? Not only was he hemiplegic, but he also had a seizure disorder and had already undergone more surgeries than most people will in a lifetime. It's a good thing we had given up the notion that life was fair long before this. Life isn't fair. Life is just life. As usual, Adam had much to teach us about this life.

After Adam completed the chemo, the results were good. The tumor had shrunk enough to remove it, and we were lucky enough to connect with an expert in this type of surgery who had just joined the staff at Anschutz Medical Center. When we took Adam to the hospital to have the surgery, he accepted this as readily as he had the chemo. He told the doctors and nurses he was scared and asked them to pray with him. He shed some tears, but always asked others how they were doing. He taught us much about authenticity and courage. The surgery was a success, and Adam continued to pray through a recovery that included lots of visits from friends who loved him. He came home after five days in the hospital and continued to heal.

Looking back at this time, I am again so grateful to have been sober and present. I can't imagine how many times I would have turned to a glass (or bottle) of wine to deal with the stress and sadness we experienced watching Adam suffer. Instead, I prayed with Adam, and Bob and I leaned into each other for support. I will always remember Adam's cancer as an extremely painful time in our lives, but I will also remember the incredible lessons we learned from Adam about love and faith and acceptance.

He was, in a word, remarkable. We were, in a word, humbled. I gained a greater personal and profound recognition of how very important Adam and people like him are to this world.

Since then, Adam has continued the life of potential that began years ago with his first steps at Adam's Camp. He lives in his own apartment with minimal support from his service agency. He just celebrated his ten year anniversary working for ARC Thrift Stores, where he serves in the corporate office two days a week as a loss prevention associate, which is the perfect complement to his love for all things law enforcement, and works in a store assisting customers on the third day. He is in a social group with guys who get together on Saturday and Wednesday nights for activities and to share a meal together. Serving as a volunteer at a police sub-station in Denver once a week feeds his love of police. He is on the board of directors for his service agency, offering his opinions about what services are best for people like him.

Adam loves God and is a well-loved member of our church. Lately, he has been talking about becoming a monk which I assume will remain a goal in his imagination, but his email correspondence with a monk at a local Abbey has us on high alert. You just never know.

He scours the internet for new information about things that interest him all the time. Between watching re-runs of Golden Girls, his time in the community, and his active Facebook associations, he has a great life. Last summer, we took a road trip devoted to all things police. We began with a ride-along with an officer of the police department in Park City, Utah, and stopped at every small sheriff's department and police station between Park City and Glenwood Springs. Adam loved every minute of that trip, and so did we.

If you had asked me what our family vacations would be like 38 years after Adam was born, I am quite sure touring police stations across the state and country wouldn't have made the list. Little did we know what unexpected joy would follow us into this new normal we had come to embrace.

35

Growing Together

ONE OF THE great joys and challenges of my job was building and maintaining our relationship with Snow Mountain Ranch (SMR), home to our summer programs. Snow Mountain Ranch is one of two YMCA mountain resort properties in Colorado that fall under the YMCA of the Rockies umbrella. The other center is in Estes Park which is about an hour and a half northeast of Denver. Kent Meyer, the director at SMR, and I became fast friends as we shared the vision of strengthening families through both our programs.

By the time Adam's Camp decided it needed more space for therapy programs and families in 1992, we had become the second largest group client at SMR. After six years of Adam's Camp at SMR, our greatest facility need was more therapy space and storage for our equipment. SMR was also growing and had priorities for expansion, so they were always looking for new ways to expand their facility.

While our growth was slow but steady over our first ten years, our trajectory began to take off around the time I became director and hired more staff. We dug our heels in and prepared to meet the need we saw in our community.

Between 1997 and 2000, the number of Therapy Campers we were serving increased by 50% while the number of Adventure Campers tripled. In 2003, we broke our Therapy Camps into Pathfinder Therapy (for younger kids) and Trailblazer Therapy (at transition program to Adventure Camp). We added programming for Adventure Campers during the year, including a Fall Retreat Week, a dance in January, and a getaway weekend in the summer.

Our need for more therapy space became more crucial when our programs began to grow so rapidly. Adam's Camp was already occupying most of the cabins and meeting space available during the weeks we held camp. We needed both additional meeting space and more lodging for our families.

Since we were in the midst of a resort community there were many condos and townhomes that often sat vacant during the summer months in the adjoining towns. Lodging was available at a reasonable rate not far from SMR. Our families could easily stay off site in one of these available properties.

Securing the needed meeting space for therapy was our greatest challenge. This space had to be on grounds so we could access all the activities available for our campers.

Was there a way we could design and build a building to suit our needs that could also be used by SMR when we were not using it?

Ideally, the building we desired would be close to our home base, built to our specifications and would be available to us at no charge whenever we were at SMR. Kent and I discussed this and agreed to present a proposal to the YMCA Board that would benefit both our organizations. Adam's Camp would raise the money to build this facility in exchange for:

- Input on the design and location of the building, which would include a storage area and an office for exclusive use by Adam's Camp
- Naming rights for the building
- Free use of an eight-bedroom family reunion cabin for two weeks each summer for thirty years

Essentially, the agreement amounts to pre-paid rent for us as well as the rights to determine location, design and free use of the building.

This arrangement works well for us as we do not want to actually own and maintain buildings at SMR. We only use these facilities five weeks out of the year, so owning makes no financial sense. Through this arrangement, however, we have exclusive use of the facility while we are at SMR, but the Y maintains it year-round and has it available to rent to other groups the rest of the year. It's a win-win.

Because of our strong partnership, the YMCA Board approved this unusual agreement. Kent and I met regularly at a Denny's midway between SMR and Denver for the next seven years to discuss fundraising strategy for this building before we actually raised the $175,000 to build it.

One of our board members at the time had been an executive with McDonald's and was able to help us secure a grant for $25,000 from the Ronald McDonald Foundation to build a handicap accessible playground. The one caveat was we had to have a full-sized figure of Ronald McDonald sitting on a bench on the playground. It was widely believed that Ronald did not blend well with the mountain ambiance, but the kids who were not freaked out by him seemed to like him. He disappeared about five years after the playground was built, and no one inquired about his whereabouts. To this day, we have no idea what happened to him.

In 2000, we cut the ribbon on this new therapy space and playground, which our Board elected to name Adam's Camp Summit. It was gratifying to have our name on a building at SMR as Adam's Camp Summit became our main therapy building. It contained a small office where we could store our equipment, which eliminated our need for the storage space we had off site. The eight-bedroom family reunion cabin we would come to call our home base was being constructed at the same time by the Y, and we were given naming rights to that as well. Independence seemed the perfect name for that building as it reflected our dream for all our special kids.

In 2016, another opportunity to enhance our programs and facilities presented itself when SMR introduced the idea of "gathering areas."

Adam's Camp provided $15,000 for an official gathering area between Independence and other cabins we used for Adventure Camp. A sturdy shelter along with a larger, permanent fire ring added a greater sense of community to what was becoming Adam's Camp's home base. Big pine Adirondack chairs, picnic tables and benches along with log bench seating at the fire ring provided a warm and welcoming outdoor venue for sing-a-longs, bar-b-ques and family meetings.

Prior to adding the gathering area, we recognized our need for still more therapy space in addition to Adam's Camp Summit.

Additionally, we wanted to expand on our dream of bringing the Adam's Camp campus together. SMR is a 5,000-acre property with buildings, cabins and lodges spread throughout. Some of the meeting rooms we were using for therapy (in addition to Adam's Camp Summit) were a few miles from our home base, Independence. Our dream included bringing all our therapy into one area.

The trust built between SMR and Adam's Camp over the years allowed us to continue to dream and build together. While both Adam's Camp and the Y had created more processes, added more staff and made more work for ourselves in the process, our partnership had grown along with us. I served on the YMCA of the Rockies Board of Directors for six years from 2002-2008, so I was familiar with and learned from much of what was happening at the time. It felt like Adam's Camp and SMR were growing up together.

After much discussion and careful consideration, it was decided by our board of directors in 2014 to take the bold step of building another space for therapy that would include a commercial kitchen and much needed storage. New layers of compliance were added by the state yearly for organizations like ours, which made the commercial kitchen necessary, but it would also be a big improvement over cooking in Independence. The YMCA was looking for a larger, nicer venue for wedding receptions, and our concept fit their needs perfectly. The land allocated for this project by the Y was just up a small hill from our current therapy space and our new gathering area. This building would put a big exclamation mark on Adam's Camp's presence at SMR and would further define our home base. And it would be expensive. By this time, the Adam's Camp budget was over $1,000,000 and we were serving over 1,000 clients per year.

We once again launched a mutually beneficial building campaign to fund this new facility at SMR. The Y agreed to split the cost of the building with Adam's Camp and we were again granted exclusive use of the building the five weeks we are there in the summer, 30 more years of two weeks free in Independence, and naming rights. Our share of this fundraising was $1,000,000.

This building campaign was much better organized than our first. We also had a larger donor base to solicit after 18 years of friend-building, as well as strong relationships with some foundations. By the end of 2014, we had pledges for over $825,000. We had come a long way from 2000 when it had taken us eight years to raise $175,000. On the strength of this commitment, we were able to break ground on this facility in 2015.

We named it Adam's Camp Promise in the spirit of the hope and promise offered our kids and families within its walls. The ribbon cutting took place in the fall of 2016, the same year we celebrated 30 years of Adam's Camp. Within over 10,000 sq. ft., Promise provides a full commercial kitchen, a large multi-use area for improved therapy spaces, accessible rest rooms and some desperately needed additional storage space to better serve our campers and staff. It is the most beautiful building on the entire property with it's rustic-elegant décor, broad beamed ceiling and beautiful views from the expansive deck.

These building projects have enhanced our little corner of Snow Mountain Ranch, where we welcome Therapy Campers, their families, and Adventure Campers alike each week of Adam's Camp. The views are spectacular, the air is clear, and the energy is palpable. Our staff, volunteers and kids come together with a greater sense of community than ever thanks to the building projects that have helped to central-ize our programs.

The people truly make the programs, but these facilities have helped us enhance the magic that is Adam's Camp for our families this one week out of the summer. One of our campers put Adam's Camp above Disney World as her favorite place to go. Now *that's* an endorsement!

36

Growing Beyond

IT WASN'T LONG after our founding that the Goode family in Nantucket heard about Adam's Camp. The Goodes had two children with Fragile X syndrome, a genetic condition which affects the X-chromosome and leads to various developmental problems like intellectual disabilities and cognitive impairment. They were continually looking for resources to help their family navigate the stressful and often lonely path they walked. Max Goode was a motivated, pro-active mom, and as soon as she learned about the therapy and support available in the magnificent Rocky Mountains at Adam's Camp, she registered her family.

The Goodes were the first of many families who would come to Adam's Camp from other states. Most of these families learned about Adam's Camp through friends or family because this onslaught began before the internet became a thing. Before we knew it, we were serving families from all over the US, including a small contingent from Alaska. A majority of our families were always from Colorado, but it has been rewarding to share the magic of Adam's Camp with folks from 37 other states.

It was natural for these families, who appreciated how much Adam's Camp helped their child and enriched their family, to dream of similar programs in their own communities. The Goodes talked to us about what it would take to start an Adam's Camp on Nantucket.

Sharing this five therapists + five campers + five days formula with as many people as we could was high on our list of priorities as an organization. We decided helping others start their own Adam's Camp programs was the best way to accomplish that goal.

When space at Snow Mountain Ranch became an obstacle to sustained growth, the decision to launch an initiative to help other groups and individuals begin their own Adam's Camps made sense. We provided them a list of 12 criteria for using our name, and also offered feet-on-the-ground support for their first three years. We would provide a consultant as well as therapists to lead the teams for these startups. This framework established Adam's Camp Outreach.

Nantucket became the pilot Outreach project. My husband, Bob, was involved in a start-up company at the time, but he had the interest and energy to oversee Outreach as a volunteer. Max Goode was the organizer and our liaison in Nantucket, and her energy and enthusiasm played a huge role in getting this program off the ground.

Max introduced us to a number of professionals on the island who worked in the special needs field. During a visit to Nantucket in the quiet winter of 2007, Bob and I had the privilege of meeting an incredible host of dedicated, kind, excited partners. Their passion for serving our special kids was inspiring, and they were equally inspired by Adam's Camp and the work we were doing

In June of 2008, Adam's Camp Nantucket was launched with ten enthusiastic families, ten skilled therapists and a host of volunteers. Instead of mountain activities, Adam's Camp Nantucket relied on the ocean and beach to provide therapeutic experiences for the campers. Nantucket provided beautiful respite opportunities for parents as well. Parent sailing day was a huge hit.

Any concerns we had about translating the Adam's Camp culture of family focused, transparent, open communication were laid to rest thanks to the genuine team of Nantucket folks who implemented the program supported by the Adam's Camp therapists and staff. All the wonder and hope of Adam's Camp showed up on the beach in the same way it did in the mountains.

Adam's Camp Nantucket has since become Adam's Camp New England. They have opened a second sight in the White Mountains of New Hampshire and continue to grow their programs to meet the needs of a growing population of kids with special needs in New England.

In 2010, we welcomed a family from Anchorage, Alaska, to Adam's Camp Colorado. After soaking in the therapy and respite, they began to dream the same dream the Goodes had. Doug and Margaret Kossler, whose son Logan has autism, joined forces with Adam's Camp and began the challenging job of finding a location, therapists, lodging and volunteers to launch our next Outreach project, which was located at a ski resort in Girdwood, about 30 minutes outside Anchorage. Again, Bob and two of our seasoned therapists supported Alaska's first camp which proved successful on all counts.

Alaska still has some very rural communities, and word of mouth brought a 12-year-old boy and his mother from a remote fishing village to camp in Girdwood in their second year of operation. This young boy had autism and had never spoken. At camp, thanks to the work of the team of therapists and especially the speech therapist, the week ended with him telling his mother he loved her. Powerful, positive outcomes like these kept Adam's Camp Alaska serving their campers with Autism for the following seven years.

By the 2000s, Adam's Camp had an active website which meant it would surely attract attention from outside the US. To our knowledge, there is still no program anywhere in the world that provides the therapy, family and sibling support and respite with the intensive attention Adam's Camp does. In 2014, a mom in Northern Ireland named Grainne Ashe found Adam's Camp online and woke her husband in the middle of the night to tell him they must take their beautiful, autistic daughter, Rose, to Adam's Camp Nantucket the following summer.

Bob heard about Grainne and her family and learned they had had an incredible experience at camp. That was all the motivation Bob needed to call Grainne and ask her if she would like to start a camp in Northern Ireland. After some hesitation, Grainne jumped in with both feet to launch a very successful program in Northern Ireland that is still serving campers with autism and their families today (2020). Bob and I enjoyed a special week touring Ireland, and he stayed for Grainne's first week as Adam's Camp Director to help her begin sharing her passion for Adam's Camp with all of Ireland.

Outreach is an ongoing process. Today, Adam's Camp continues to support Adam's Camp New England and Adam's Camp Northern Ireland, although Alaska has taken a hiatus as they struggle to raise the funds necessary to run camp. Adam's Camp's Outreach efforts are currently focused on starting Early Start programs in communities outside the Denver Metro area. These programs can feed into any of the existing Adam's Camps for older kids and families as these children grow.

Bob, like me, has retired. He left a big mark on Adam's Camp with his Outreach efforts and is ingrained in the hearts of those he helped begin those programs. There is nothing quite like the beginnings of something wonderful. It's so gratifying and humbling to see the impact Adam's Camp has had on so many after providing over17,000 camper and family member experiences since 1986. We have found the cultural or regional differences between us disappear when we connect through the kids who bring us all together. Digging deep into the new and unasked for life parents of kids with special needs have been given calls for us to work hard, but also uncovers the rare beauty that can only be described by one person in our family sharing with another. Hope shared is hope multiplied, and that seems universal in this very special world of special needs.

37

...And Now?

WHILE I WAS working for Adam's Camp, I couldn't imagine my life without my job. I loved the work, the people, and the outcomes. Working 30 hours a week left me time to work out, attend AA meetings, see friends and manage life at home.

It was around the summer of 2013 I began to contemplate turning the day-to-day reigns of Adam's Camp over to someone else. Driving to and from camp ten times each summer was beginning to wear on me, and the attention to compliance, IT and the more technical tasks involved in running an ever-growing organization (my least favorite parts of the job) were taking more and more time. Managing a staff of 12 was stimulating, sometimes perplexing, and often exhausting.

I found myself talking with Bob and my friends about the "R" word more frequently. I mentioned my intention to *retire* sometime in the foreseeable future to my friend and Finance Director, Laura. As it turns out, she was thinking about cutting back or retiring as well, and we knew we both couldn't retire at the same time. We were the only two staff with long history and knowledge of the organization. I got the long straw, and we decided I would retire first.

At the board of directors retreat in November of 2013, I announced my intention to retire at the end of 2014. I agreed to stay until the board found someone to replace me and for however long it took to train that person.

It's interesting to experience the reaction to a founder leaving an organization. So much of the identity of the organization is tied to that person, it is often hard for people to imagine life after that founder. I had no such problem. I was sure there was someone out there who was more capable than I who could take Adam's Camp to new heights.

In November of 2014, the annual Adam's Camp Recognition Dinner was held in my honor. It was a thoughtful tribute that will remain one of my fondest memories. I was presented with a beautifully crafted quilt made from Adam's Camp t-shirts from over the years, and it hangs in our family room today. One of our truly dedicated families, Jim and Veronica Brennan, created a video of campers, families and volunteers thanking me for my service to Adam's Camp. A wooden plaque featuring a photo of Adam and me was presented to me by our son Jared on behalf of Adam's Camp. I was surrounded by the people I loved, many of whom had been a part of Adam's Camp since the beginning.

I felt truly honored and loved that night. I always feel honored and loved for my work with Adam's Camp. I am humbled by the amount of credit I receive for all that Adam's Camp has become because it has been shepherded by so many incredible, talented, passionate people.

The search for my replacement took about six months, and in January of 2015 a genuinely kind man who had directed a different local non-profit was hired to become the next executive director. He started work in March, and I stayed by his side for about two weeks before turning in my keys for the last time. It was bittersweet, but I was ready.

I had recently been elected to the board of our church, was going to do some consulting with an organization that served people with disabilities in our county, and remained active in AA. I was also beginning to help care for triplets who had been born to the daughter of a dear friend of mine. Yet when I packed the boxes brimming with Adam's Camp memories and walked out of the office on my final day, I could already feel the void left in my soul. I wasn't sure what my role with Adam's Camp would be in the future, and while I hoped to stay involved, that would be up to the board and the new director.

Adam's Camp has been through its ups and downs in the five years since I have been gone, but it is a strong and vital organization today. A very capable executive director succeeded the man I mentioned who left after two years to work for an organization for which he had great passion and direct ties. I am grateful for the staff and volunteers who continue to keep Adam's Camp meeting the needs of so many, but as I have witnessed two changes in leadership over the past five years, I have a much greater understanding of how much influence the leader has in shaping the culture and ultimately outcomes of the organization.

I now know I had underestimated how much I actually influenced the day to day operations because I had been around since the beginning. I was familiar with all aspects of our work because I had performed just about every job there was. It is only in retrospect that I can see where my influence shaped Adam's Camp as I watch the subtle changes that have taken place under two different leaders. Some of those changes have been great, and others have been disastrous. While it has been painful to watch Adam's Camp struggle, I know God has a plan and is continuing to carry it out. So many new and innovative programs are blossoming at Adam's Camp today, and it is a joy to meet with the current executive director to talk about the ever-evolving future of the organization. I am grateful to still attend and speak at events, meet with the current director as an advisor, and hear stories of the life-changing impact Adam's Camp continues to have on families, campers, therapists and volunteers.

When I think about my life today as I head toward the goal line, I am at perfect peace about my purpose. I know there are many who struggle with the question "Why am I here?". Not me. I am blessed to have a legacy, and while I know I have a greater purpose with my family and impact on others in recovery, I will most be remembered for founding Adam's Camp.

I know, left to my own devices, my legacy would have been

something quite different. My exhaustive search for peace, power and prestige culminated in a world of addiction and "never enough." When I used my gift of leadership for manipulation and my personality for selfish gain, pride continued to serve as my compass in life. Without the scaffolding of titles and approval, I was non-existent in my own eyes. I masked my anxiety and fear by binge drinking and eating every weekend for literally two decades of my life.

Because of my inability to conceive due to my anorexia, I underwent fertility treatments that resulted in the birth of triplets, one of whom died and one of whom has cerebral palsy as a result of prematurity. One of my sons inherited the gene of alcoholism from me and suffers from that disease today. None of my sons lives what would be considered a "normal life", and the reason for that leads directly back to a gene their mother inherited.

The trajectory of my life was heading toward destruction of my body, my family and my purpose. While I knew my pattern of living couldn't be good for my body, I had no idea what a prisoner I was to my addictions. I truly believed I could change that pattern whenever I chose to...until I couldn't. It took walking into the rooms of recovery to discover the depths of my powerlessness. I desperately needed a profound change.

Looking back, I can see how the gentle hand of God both pushed and pulled me into His embrace. I tried so desperately to cling to the control I believed was the solution to all my problems, only to return to my destructive behaviors for relief. After finally surrendering my will to the program of recovery, I found myself gradually turning toward God. In the beginning, God walked behind me where I could turn around and ask for his help when I thought I needed it. After recognizing that He seemed to enhance my problem-solving, I decided to ask him to walk beside me; serve as my partner. I thought we would make a great team. Eventually, I came to believe He actually had BETTER plans than I did and that my only real purpose was to put Him ahead of me and make an effort to follow Him. That is when my life truly changed.

I know I am one of the lucky ones. According to the Centers for

Disease Control and Prevention, up to 14 million adult drinkers in the United States are estimated to abuse alcohol each year. That amounts to approximately 1 in every 13 adults in this country. It appears that only about 16 percent of those who need treatment ever actually receive it, and of those, recovery rates at the one-year marker are estimated at 35.9 percent. In my experience, the success rate drops from there, even after a year of sobriety. Nothing brings these statistics into clearer view for me than watching my son Jared struggle to get and stay sober.

So why me? Why do I have the life I have today when so many others never find the freedom I have been given? It certainly has nothing to do with me being a better or stronger person. The truth is, I don't know why I have been given the life I have. But I do know this.

I am free today. I have peace and capacity to love. My past is forgiven and my goals are simply to follow the path God has prepared for me. My ultimate goal is to know Him better, to continue to become the authentic woman He created me to be. I thank God daily for giving me a supportive husband, loving kids and phenomenal friends. I have the privilege of loving and sharing life with three "adopted" grandkids who fill my life with joy. I thank God for allowing me to fulfill His purpose with Adam's Camp, knowing He could have chosen anyone to do this work.

Recovery remains a priority for me. I participate in service work on the board of my Recovery Club. I work with other women, sharing the program I have been so freely given. I belong and serve in a church that embraces the message of love and grace that saved my life. I love to talk to God in nature through cycling and walking.

I am far from perfect. I still am not a big fan of house guests, have much to learn about accepting people who don't do things the way I think they should and have to work at being flexible because I know I can become way too comfortable with my routine. I am a work in progress, and I am just fine with that. God created all of us to be works in progress.

I'm pretty sure God is not finished with me yet. Each day, He reveals something new about Himself to me which seems to reveal something new about myself to me as well. The recognition that the more I see, the less I know makes me excited to see what's in store. If the past is any indication, I had better buckle up.

With gratitude to those who allowed me to lean into them to create this book.....

Judy, my friend and editor without whom I would never have embarked on this daunting journey. I am so grateful for your expertise, unwavering encouragement and love.

Dianna, whose cover design of this book represents her incredible talent as well as a precious friendship that spans decades. You are truly one in a million.

Shari Caudron, whose thoughtful guidance helped me add life to these pages.

My writer friend and Adam's Camp cohort Jenni, who took the time to read and critique this book. Thank you for your insight from the viewpoint of my partner, coworker and beloved friend.

The men and women of AA, without whom this story would read very differently. You ground and humble me daily with your courage and wisdom.

The remarkable, talented, selfless people who are Adam's Camp. I was flat out blessed to work with each of you, volunteer and staff alike. I'm sure you have no idea what a gift you are!

The men and women of Colorado Community Church who continue to reveal genuine love the way Christ intended. My faith is fueled by your example.

My family. Loving, thoughtful, supportive, funny, and fiercely loyal. You are so much of who I have become.

CPSIA information can be obtained
at www.ICGtesting.com
Printed in the USA
FSHW011919201020
74909FS